# VISIONS OF ARARAT
*Writings on Armenia*

Christopher J. Walker

D1472008

## I.B. TAURIS

LONDON · NEW YORK

New edition published in 2005
by I.B.Tauris & Co. Ltd.
6 Salem Road, London W2 4BU
175 Fifth Avenue, New York, NY 10010

In the United States of America and Canada distributed by
St Martin's Press, 175 Fifth Avenue, New York, NY 10010

A full CIP record for this book is available
from the British Library

ISBN 1 85043 888 9
EAN 978 1 85043 888 5

Set in Monotype Baskerville by Philip Armstrong, Sheffield
Updated in 2005 by Avon DataSet Ltd, Bidford on Avon, Warwickshire
Printed and bound in Great Britain by TJ International Ltd, Padstow, Cornwall

# CONTENTS

PREFACE

'When Harry met Harutiun ...'; this book records a number of encounters between Britons and Armenians. The English studied or visited Armenia for a wide variety of reasons – scholastic, journalistic, theological, itinerant. The focus here is on the Armenians they came across. What sort of people were they? It becomes pretty clear that they had widely dissimilar characteristics, making it hard to speak of the Armenian character. Armenian lives and experiences are too varied to be accommodated under one rubric.

Perhaps the search for national character is no more than a kind of nineteenth-century after-dinner pastime. The search to identify a patronizing stereotype unravels as an attempt to gratify our own superiority and brilliantly subtle capacity at categorizing other peoples; an activity which we hardly notice borders on the racist. Maybe the most one can say is that there are certain 'sides' to a national character, or that a certain amount of statistical clumping occurs around certain activities. No other significant conclusion can be drawn.

If national character withers under the spotlight of anti-racism and of the idea of the brotherhood of humankind, national geography remains uncompromisingly factual; it has been the mortar in which national culture has been fashioned, and has built the scenery of national history. Armenian geography is characterized by the harsh yet spirit-elevating terrain of high mountain chains and deep valleys, which burst forth into momentous summers and fold back into implacably hard winters. Armenian culture, rich and diverse, is the product of language, literacy, religious faith, geographical and economic facts, and social organization. If we look carefully at an Armenian church, built compactly from the fine local stone, as if indicating that the faith is both private and natural (yet broad when seen from within), or if we scrutinize a manuscript illumination, highlighting a Gospel event and painted in a rich and passionately engaged Eastern manner, we at once assent to their being Armenian. Judgments become possible about things which are less easy with people. The attempt to pin down a national character draws us back to geography, culture and the uncompromising facts of history.

There is a further element here. People ill-disposed towards Armenia and Armenians have sought to downgrade, denigrate, and ignore the country and her people. Armenia fits awkwardly, if at all, into the schematization of any number of grand strategists and saloon-bar academics. She is an Eastern but Christian country, whose flowering as a Christian civilization dates from the time when the Eastern Mediterranean was the central locus of literate faith, and 'the West' was locked in barbarian darkness. Armenia gained her alphabet in the same century in which Rome collapsed under barbarism. Today she constitutes an uneasy puzzle for two sets of people: first, those with simplistic minds who believe that 'the west' is coterminous with Christianity and 'the east' with Islam, and that there is a more or less perpetual undeclared war between the two, when factual history teaches us about Asiatic Christian civilization; and second, those who accept the current illiberal, anti-human schematization of politics foisted on the world by intelligence departments and proponents of the fantasy of 'global terrorism', which leads to a world structure which, in its rush to embrace corporate-like states, ignores historical truths, regional disputes, or smaller nations. But these deviations may not last for ever.

Thus the historic accounts of travellers, war correspondents, clergymen, scholars and geographers have a significance beyond the facts which they were carefully laying out to their public at the time. Today they constitute political events, demonstrations even, standing in defiant opposition to the shuffling evasive silence and ideological airbrushing engineered by the 'new world order' (which, in its cousinage to Metternich or Castlereagh, is in fact quite old).

Armenia responded to the humane, just, quiet and dissenting side of the English character, which emerged decisively in the nineteenth century. She did not find common ground with the imperial, commanding, controlling or intriguing side of our nationality. A congenial spirit was recognized when any scholarly, curious, sympathetic and unbigoted Englishman or woman visited her; and her cause lost out when the England of empire and world-pretensions started to demand attention; when the feverish paranoid defensiveness of a feared imperial attack was fantastically presented. She never took kindly to the boot-prints of imperial arrogance.

Just as, in the days of the Cold War, it wasn't quite cricket for a westerner to say anything too favourable about Armenia, so in the long nineteenth century, from 1791 to 1914, to express interest in Armenia, or to voice sympathy for her historic issues, was to invite a slur of pro-Russianism, a hint of traitorousness, at a time when Russia was the great imperial rival of Britain. Gladstone was upbraided for being unpatriotic by Queen Victoria, an arch-hater of Eastern Christians. Even now, well over a decade since the fall of the Soviet Union, Armenians are still compelled to campaign to have the facts of their own history, as observed by outsiders, accepted as true. It does not seem to be apparent to those who, knowing better, allow themselves to utter falsehoods about Armenia, or airbrush her from history, that they are doing the kind of job *Pravda* did at the height of the Cold War.

It remains to add some points which amplify the study of Britain and Armenia. The first concerns the development of Armenian studies in England in the seventeenth century. Armenian studies began in England with Edward Brerewood's *Enquiries* of 1614, and continued in Ephraim Pagitt's *Christianography* of 1639. Both these books constitute flawed efforts at discovering truthful facts. When in the late 1630s Archbishop Laud attempted to create a unity of the Anglican and Eastern Churches he founded a structure of systematic learning and research about the East. Laud's legacy of interest in the region drew Dudley Loftus from Dublin to Oxford, where, in the ferment of Oriental studies which developed there in the years immediately before the English Civil War, he became the first important Armenian scholar from the British Isles. Some of his books may be found today in Marsh's Library in Dublin.

During the Commonwealth the English Polyglot Bible was produced, a massive work in six volumes and nine languages. The editors hoped to include an Armenian Bible text, but their working manuscript was too badly damaged. Politically the main importance of the Polyglot lay in the opposition to it from the Puritans, specifically from John Owen, Oxford's vice-chancellor. He declared that the Holy Bible should not be compared in its different versions. To do so was to call into question its providential nature. Like Southern Baptists today in the United States, and biblical reactionary fundamentalists everywhere, Owen declared that the Bible should not be seen as a created thing. Textual criticism was akin to blasphemy. This ignorant and bigoted viewpoint – a summation of all that Erasmus had struggled against – effectively leads to the outlawing of any comparative study of religious texts, and the end of any kind of theological tolerance and research.

The final point is the issue of nationalism. Armenian nationalism is again being blamed for the catastrophes of the Armenians in the Ottoman empire in the late nineteenth and early twentieth centuries. Two points should be made here. The first is that, in almost all cases, the Ottoman government was the instigator of oppression and violence. Ottoman rule has been portrayed as meek and ineffectual, a lazy declawed tiger rolling over on its back. This picture is quite false. The rule of law did not exist for Armenians in the Ottoman provinces. They were

denied legal redress for crimes committed by their non-Armenian
neighbours. Generalized political thuggery descended into pogrom.
Sultan Abdul Hamid II was driven by extreme and destructive political-
religious sentiments; and the atheist Young Turks who took power in 1908,
after an initial six months of genuine equality, subsided into a bleak
intolerance which grew ever more brutal, eventually bringing about the
massive suppression of the non-Turkish peoples of the Anatolian empire.

Secondly, the Armenians for their part would have preferred not to
have been nationalist. Two of their favourite writers, Hagop Baronian and
Yervant Odian, wrote hilariously of the conflict between the old ways of
the Ottoman Armenian village and the new ideas picked up mostly from
the Russian opponents of the St Petersburg autocracy (Armenia was
divided between the two empires). Unfortunately Armenia lay in the way
of the Turkish 'blue-sky' thinkers of the day, with the expected outcome.
That savage consequence must surely be another reason to defy the
bureaucrats of power and to assert proudly the past history and present
reality of Armenia.

I am grateful to various friends for their advice and help. I thank the
librarians of the British Library, Lambeth Palace Library, the London
Library, and my local Hammersmith Public Library. I owe acknow-
ledgements to Cambridge University Press for allowing me to reproduce
sections of *Caucasian Battlefields* by W. E. D. Allen and Paul Muratoff, to
Save the Children for the right to use Dr Armstrong Smith's report of
1922, and to the author and HarperCollins for permission to reproduce
the extract from *The Crossing Place* by Philip Marsden.

The Republic of Armenia

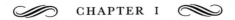

## CHAPTER I

# 'From the Remotest Times'

### (I) ANTIQUITY AND THE MIDDLE AGES

The most significant geographical feature of Armenia is its mountains. They buttress it to the north and south, creating an elevated plateau, which forms a natural fortress with a climate so fierce that no invading army has ever been tempted to linger long. In good times the Armenian people lived with their own social organization, their princes and some-times their monarchy; but foreign empires often coveted control of the territory, and the land became divided between the realms of others. Despite loss of sovereignty the majority of Armenians kept their language, faith, traditions and culture. Steadfastness, and even stubbornness, have long been noted as qualities observable among the people.

They are an ancient people, mentioned by Herodotus and Xenophon, and in an inscription of the Persian king Darius, dating from 530 BC. In their mountainous homeland they have survived continuously to this day on their own soil, despite war, invasion and massacre. Their language, Armenian, is Indo–European, akin to most European tongues today, and to Iranian. (It is quite distinct from either Turkish, which is known to specialists as an 'agglutinative' language, or Arabic and Hebrew, which are Semitic.)

Are the Armenians European or Asiatic? Since their homeland is east of Asia Minor, and their present capital is on almost the same longitude as Baghdad, it is not easy to call them European. Only by deft manip-ulation of continental borders can Armenia be included in Europe. Yet Armenians feel a strong cultural pull towards Europe – although their own culture partakes of a number of Asiatic features.

Europe or Asia? How can one resolve the conundrum? Maybe a clue can be found from a better knowledge and understanding of history, especially by considering the long, and long-neglected, centuries of the civilization of Byzantium and its neighbours. For if we give a Byzantine perspective to Armenian history, rather than a modern western European one, we can see that for centuries Asia Minor was the heart of the civilized world. To come from Asia Minor, or virtually any Mediterranean or near-Mediterranean country, and to be cultured were practically synonymous – rather in the same way that 'western European' (or 'western') and 'civilized' have been allowed to become synonymous today. Armenia grew to statehood on the eastern edge of Byzantium, and discovered the arts of writing, literature and architecture when such skills were prized in the Byzantine empire but largely dormant in western Europe. Armenia carries its civilization from distant centuries, when the world's cultural configuration was different from that of today. It is therefore hard to find a European home for Armenia, unless 'Europe' is used as a synonym for 'civilized'.

Armenia drew some of its culture from the east. When, in antiquity, it was situated between Rome and Parthia, faith and culture came from both its neighbours. But Armenia at one stage transformed itself into one of the empires typical of its neighbours; in 69 BC the Armenian empire under King Tigran ruled a large part of eastern and central Anatolia and the Caucasus, before being subdued by Rome.

In terms of the country's subsequent history, the most important event of the early period was the adoption of Christianity as the state religion, probably in the year 301. Christianity had reached Armenia somewhat earlier; according to tradition, the apostles St Thaddeus and St Bartholemew had themselves spread the gospel in Armenia; therefore the Armenian Church is of apostolic origin, and so its correct title today is the 'Armenian Apostolic Church'. Armenia's acceptance of Christianity predated that of the Roman empire.

About 100 years later a devout scribe invented an alphabet which exactly matched the sounds of the Armenian language, giving the nation the gift of literacy. The first texts to be translated and written in the new script were the bible and the liturgy. With the combination of faith and literacy, the Armenians emerged as a nation equipped for the future. Their individuality and uniqueness was further stressed when their church began to separate from the main branch of orthodoxy, in the fifth century AD. This was a time of major disputes about the nature of Christ, coinciding with a conflict about the authority of the individual churches. A church council was held at Chalcedon, to discuss the humanity and the divinity of Christ, in the year 451. On matters both of dogma and of jurisdiction the Armenian Church rejected the conclusions of this council, and 100 years later established itself as a fully separate church, with its own calendar. Even today, the Armenian Church dates its documents from the year 551.

Stirring deeds strengthened the faith and tempered the national consciousness, notably the battle of Avarayr (whose site is now in Iran), which
took place in the same year as the Council of Chalcedon, and in which
the Armenians fought against the Sasanian Persians for the right to believe
in their new Christian faith. This battle, though militarily a defeat for the
Armenians, was politically and indeed spiritually a great victory, since it
came to be viewed as a noble defeat, in the same sense that Christ's death
on the Cross had been a defeat, a defeat that presaged a resurrection.
Avarayr was of deep symbolic significance for a people that was now
imbued to a very deep level with the faith of the Cross. The battle of
Avarayr, victory in defeat, fired the imagination of all the people and
united them around the twin ideas of faith and nation.

The Armenian ruling dynasties existed somewhat precariously in
antiquity and late antiquity, since their nation was located between the
powers, latterly, of Byzantium and the Arab Caliphate. Any great power
could be intent on control and aggrandizement, and the Christian
Byzantines showed themselves to be no less so than the Muslim Arabs.
Armenians found that their most productive and peaceful times were
when the local empires were weak, giving them a wide measure of
autonomy. Some of their finest churches, a number of which are still
standing today, date from the period of the Bagratid monarchy (AD 886–
1064), when the Armenian kingdom was recognized by both Byzantine
emperor and the Muslim caliph. A remarkable, flourishing medieval
civilization established itself at this time in the Armenian highlands. Its
capital Ani ranked with Constantinople and Baghdad as one of the few
great cities of the medieval world. Ani's magnificent ruins can still be seen
today, located in eastern Turkey, actually on the border with Armenia.

Ani remained the Armenian capital until the late eleventh century. It
fell partly because the Byzantines desired military conquest and the
subordination of border regions rather than the establishment of local
support in distant provinces; and partly as a result of an irruption of the
Seljuk Turks under the leadership of Alp Arslan. Despite Greater
Armenia's loss of independence, life and culture flowered anew in an
Armeno–Georgian state established at the time of Georgian Queen
Tamara and her successors. Many of the finest stone crosses, or khachkars,
that one sees strewn around Armenia today, with almost reckless abandon,
date from the thirteenth and fourteenth centuries. Even after the extinction
of sovereignty, the people lived on in their ancient highlands, partly
adapting, but keeping their villages, monasteries and even some of their
old social organization. These things kept alight the flame of Armenian
nationhood, when the princes were no more.

## Cilicia

Despite the fall of the Bagratid kingdom and its successor, the nation re-emerged, first as a barony and then a monarchy, in Cilicia (central southern Turkey today, just north from Cyprus). Cilicia had been alternately Byzantine, then Muslim from the seventh century, then Byzantine again following the conquests of Nicephorus Phocas (965). Armenians moved here and into adjoining regions in two waves: first just after the Byzantine re-conquest, and second after the fall of Ani and the loss of sovereignty in the Armenian highlands. An Armenian chieftain was able to establish his rule over a large part of the region of the Taurus for about a decade in the late eleventh century. Part of this state then fell to two Turkish tribes, the Seljuks and the Danishmendids, part to Baldwin of Boulogne and other crusaders; but perhaps most importantly, Armenian Cilicia was also formed out of it. This state was led for about 150 years by the Roupen family, then for a century by the rival Hetum dynasty, and finally, for its last 50 years, by a dynasty of European origin. In virtually every respect it became the new Armenia. The head of the church, the catholicos, left the Caucasus, and travelled with his flock to their new home by the Mediterranean.

Despite political uncertainty, Armenia experienced a Silver Age in Cilicia. Here the nation first made contact with Christian Europe, and found much common cause with the crusaders, usually (but not always) giving support to the crusading armies. Contact with Europe stimulated a new direction for the faith and culture and general outlook of the Armenians. Hitherto Armenia had seen its faith as a great inner spiritual blessing. There is no doubt that this view continued in Cilicia; writings by the great church leaders of the time, notably Nerses Shnorhali, the spiritual head of the church in the early twelfth century, testify to that. Moreover Armenians from all over the land, in the Armenians highlands themselves, recognized the spiritual primacy of the church then in its Cilician home.

But religious beliefs became entwined with political aspirations, and European issues. The Armenian world view became changed. Not least of the elements in that change was the powerful and persistent pressure on the Armenians to 'latinize' and recognize not their own catholicos but the pope of Rome as spiritual head. There was not a little slippage towards Rome, from monarchs hard pressed by allies to convert. But the popular mood was against Rome. A smouldering atmosphere of revolt was commonplace. In the process Cilician Armenia ultimately lost her medieval statehood, but Armenians held on to the freedom to maintain their identity, and to an important ecclesiastical notion: their direct spiritual lineage from Christ's own apostles, unmediated by any other church authority.

In an age of faith, deeds comprehensible only in terms of faith are performed. But the refracted light of faith may change in changing times. Cilician Armenia appears, while holding to the same faith as the Bagratid monarchy, to have found a new emphasis for its Christianity. The faith which had operated diplomatically in the regions around Ani and Van, and which had sought to preserve the nation balanced between large powers, lost some of its subtlety in Cilicia. The Armenians perceived opportunities and devised plans which were not always proportional to the nation's real strength.

The spirit of the times encouraged the Armenians to believe that their future was assured. This was symbolized by the creation in 1199 of the Armenian monarchy of Cilicia. In that year Prince Levon II was crowned in a splendid ceremony in the cathedral of Tarsus, to become King Levon I. (The Cilician kings are however known more by their princely than royal titles, so he is more familiarly known as Levon, or Leo, II.) The papal legate, Conrad of Hildesheim, was present, presenting insignia from the Holy Roman Emperor. Levon was keener that his coronation should be witnessed by a European representative than by an emissary from Byzantium. This signalled the tilt of allegiances.

The state reached a remarkable level of culture and prosperity. Her national ideals developed as appropriate rather more to those of feudal Christian Europe of the time, and less to those of the Caucasian milieu in which she had existed in the Armenian mountains. Chief of the new set of ideals was a warlike posture adopted from the example of the Frankish armies, who in turn were responding as much to land-hunger in Europe, and the crisis of European feudalism, as to the call of the faith of Christ. If the battle of Avarayr had for the Armenians ennobled a vision of Christian martyrdom, in Cilicia the nation sought Christian victory. Avarayr and its victory-in-defeat might have puzzled some Armenians in Cilician times. The concerns of Europe, and the straight-forward politics of the Franks – the collective name for western Europeans in the Levant – dominated Armenia's situation until the end of the fourteenth century.

As the confidence of Cilician Armenians was growing, bolstered by alliances with such powers as the Mongols of remotest Asia (by whom they sought to outflank Islam), so the actual political circumstances, and the options in the Levant, were diminishing. Even before the coronation of Levon at Tarsus, Saladin had reconquered Jerusalem. The crusades began to lose their momentum; by the mid thirteenth century, the fierce inner spirit which drove them had become weakened. Egypt, hitherto ruled by the non-belligerent Shiite Fatimids, became dominated first by the Sunni Ayyubids, then by the more belligerent Mamluks. In Europe, spiritual rewards were promised for less arduous tasks than crusading in Syria.

Despite the precariousness of its alliances, and the virtual encirclement of Cilicia by hostile forces, Cilician Armenia showed evidence of progress and consolidation. Marco Polo, who travelled to Cilicia in 1271, found a fine and busy port there, at Ayas, or Lajazzo. Finished goods from Europe were traded for exotic wares from the Caspian region and Central Asia. Medicine, law, sacred poetry and miniature painting were all encouraged, and were often seen to flourish, in Cilician times. The works of St Thomas Aquinas were translated into Armenian. But the political and military options were narrowing. Cilicia's flowering was brief, before the clouds grew squally. The barony was made into a monarchy as its enemies were growing more powerful, and by 1375 Cilician Armenia was no more. It has bequeathed to the present some fine castles, and magnificent illuminated manuscripts, but no churches or palaces. Until the First World War its highlands preserved the ancient spirit of Armenian autonomy and self-rule among the inhabitants of the remote Cilician towns of Zeitun and Hadjin, places almost too inaccessible for empires to impose their control. As well as in these towns, there lived in lowland Cilicia hundreds of thousands of Armenians, whose roots dated back a thousand years or so. Only the tragic events during and after the war of 1914–18 ended all Armenian habitation of Cilicia.

## (II) BELOVED FELLOW-BROTHER LEO: EARLY ENGLISH CONTACTS

England and Armenia first made contact with one another when the two nations were individually strong, although the situation in the east, following Saladin's reconquest of Jerusalem, was unpromising. The background was that of the Third Crusade. In May 1191 Richard Coeur de Lion, one of the most dedicated crusading knights, as well as one of the most uncompromising, arrived in Cyprus; he expelled the Byzantine governor and ruled the island, initiating over 300 years of Frankish rule. Richard married Princess Berengaria of Navarre there too; one of the chief guests at his wedding was King Levon II of Cilician Armenia. Levon also fought alongside Richard at the siege of Acre in July.

For a century thereafter there is little evidence of contact between the two nations. But in 1291, Acre fell to the Muslim armies, and the following year the Armenian citadel of Hromkla, the seat of the head of the Armenian church, was taken by the Egyptian Mamluks.

The times were not good for Cilicia, and other powers, spiritual and temporal, sought to help. Contacts developed in both directions between England and Armenia. In 1298, the pope sent an exhortation to Edward I, requesting assistance for the king of Armenia.[1] In 1307 the Armenian king Hetum II sent a three-man delegation to England, composed of Baldewynus (that is, Baldwin – the Armenian nobility had begun to adopt European names) and Toros, both from the monastery of Trazark in Cilicia, and an officer named Leo.[2] Edward I had died, and Edward II was on the throne, a monarch who sought to maintain but not initiate crusading policy. He ordered the garrison at Dover to give free passage to the delegation, and to treat them with the honour due, and he granted them a bursary of 50 sterling marks.[3]

The kings of Cilician Armenia and England corresponded throughout the fourteenth century. Edward II recommended William, 'episcopus Liddensis', to Levon IV in November 1307, on the occasion of the bishop's travels to the region, requesting Levon's hospitality.[4] Edward III ordered 40 lb. of silver to be given to the 'nunciis de Ermonye', in December 1335.[5] In 1342 the monarchical line died out and the Armenian nobility offered the crown to the Lusignan family.

It was accepted by Guy de Lusignan, who ruled for two years with the title Constantine II. He was a brave warrior, but the factionalism and intrigues which characterized his reign led inevitably to weakness. He was also a Catholic, and a latinizer. He surrounded himself with French speakers, and Europeanized his court. To the populace he seemed to be leading his nation far from its mountainous, Caucasian origin.

Relations however remained good between the Armenians under the Lusignans and the English during the reign of Edward III. Documents tell us that Armenian monks travelled to England in 1360 to collect funds to repair churches;[6] and in 1364 a certain bishop Nerses, with Hagop, one of his monks, was permitted to travel throughout England on a pilgrimage. The text of the letter emphasized the sorrowful state of conditions in Cilicia: its people slaughtered without distinction of rank, sex or age, and its sanctuaries profaned.[7]

The Egyptian Mamluks were all the time gaining in confidence and ability. Soon they were at the gates of Cilicia's heartland. The last king of Armenia, Levon VI, ruled for two brief periods, in 1363–64 and in 1374–75, before his kingdom was overrun. He was taken prisoner to Cairo, along with his queen, Margaret of Soissons, and their two children.

Levon was released from Cairo after seven years' detention. He travelled to Europe, seeking European help to regain his kingdom and defend his people. But the fragile unity created by the crusades (which indeed had rapidly developed into a western European enterprise rather than a Christian one, as was shown by the attitude of the crusaders to the Byzantine empire) was a thing of the past. England and France were immersed in the Hundred Years' War.

Despite the bleak outlook, ex-king Levon worked for a rapprochement between the warring parties, and sought peace between them. He was granted an audience with Charles VI of France in June 1384. In a speech the Armenian king offered to undertake mediation.[8] He put himself forward to the French nobility as neutral outsider, and his offer appears to have been accepted. Levon communicated his intention of mediation to England's Richard II. Richard issued letters patent for Levon:

> The king to all his admirals etc. Salutation. Be it known to you that when the illustrious Prince Levon, king of the Armenians, reaches our English soil, in order that he might come and return in safety, with this letter we take under our protection the king with his subjects and servants ... of every rank, with forty horses and all their armour, all the time he is on our soil, on sea or on land, from the time he comes until he returns freely ...[9]

A similar letter was issued for 'John de Rousp, the high seneschal of the illustrious prince, Leo, king of the Armenians, in company with five people, six horses, four archers, 24 bearded subjects, with all their equipage.'[10]

With these letters, the former Armenian monarch and his party arrived at Dover, towards the end of 1385. According to Froissart, their arrival caused some panic at the port, since a French landing was expected. They were nevertheless entertained handsomely, being duly met by many barons and 3,000 infantry. English suspicion persisted, and only the authority of the earl of Buckingham allowed the ex-king to travel on to London.

Froissart's account tells us that, when he arrived in the capital, 'he was much stared at by Londoners: the better sort, however, showed him every honour and respect.' His presence engendered further anxiety about a French invasion. But the king and his council assembled in Westminster, and listened to what the Armenian monarch had to say: an 'elegant harangue' according to Froissart.[11] Another chronicler tells us that Levon said: 'The hostilities between the two nations have lasted too long. I think that it is necessary to implore the two rivals to be content with their extensive domains, and to bring to an end the war between their subjects.'[12] In reply, according to Froissart, the archbishop of Canterbury declared that he took the ex-king's points, but that Levon should be directing all his energies towards France, and that peace depended upon the French pulling back their forces.

Richard II appears to have struck up almost a friendship with Levon, and to have shown rather more willingness to take the Armenian's message to heart. But no agreement was concluded, since there was no general political will for reconciliation. The chronicler Holinshed summed up the situation thus:

This yeare [1385] king Richard holding his Christmasse at Eltham, thither came to him Leo king of Armenia, whose countrie and realme being in danger to be conquered of the Turks, he was come into those west parts of christendome for aid and succour at the hands of the christian princes here. The king honorablie receiued him, and after he had taken counsell touching his request, he gaue him great summes of monie and other rich gifts, with a stipend (as some write) of a thousand pounds yearely to be paid to him during his life. After he had remained here two moneths space, he tooke leaue of the king and departed. The chiefest point of his errand was, to haue procured a peace betwixt the two kings of England and France, but destinie would not permit so good a purpose to take effect: for the hatred which either nation bare to other, would not suffer their loftie minds to yeeld in any one point, further than seemed good in their owne opinion.[13]

The popularity of the war gave no chance to reconciliation. Richard's generous grant of money was decreed 'half at Easter and half at Michaelmas, until he be able to repossess his kingdom with the help of God'.[14]

Perhaps Levon returned to England. But if he did, he would not have remained for long, since he died in Paris on 29 November 1393, and was buried with due pomp in St Denys. Levon's last link with England was his will, in which he appointed Richard II, along with the king of Castile, as executors.

So ended a strange and rather moving episode of attempted peace-making. Levon VI was the first and last Armenian king to come to England. His arrival in Europe derived from the Armenian policy of securing alliances with the European nations which Levon II had initiated two centuries earlier. He sought to re-kindle the crusading enterprise, and to regain his throne and thereby to strengthen his nation; peace-making in Europe was part of a strategy aimed at both these objectives. It failed, partly because Armenians, at that time and later, did not grasp the nature of the divisions which existed in Christian Europe; and partly because the Armenians gave greater importance to long-distance alliances than to local ones. But however one views the actions of the last king of Armenia, whether as self-interest or a vain attempt to recreate a unity in Christendom which had been questionable from the outset, and often little more than an opportunistic alliance, they are surely praiseworthy as an early effort to build an Entente Cordiale.

Perhaps echoing the interest in things Armenian at the time, there is, in an English poem of the late fourteenth century, a story about an Armenian princess. The poem is John Gower's *Confessio Amantis* (The Lover's Confession) which was written probably in 1383 or 1384, during the reign of Richard II, to whom it is dedicated. At this time the Armenian ex-king was seeking reconciliation within Europe.

*Confessio Amantis* takes the form of a series of moral tales showing the pitfalls of making the wrong judgement in love. Book Four concerns sloth, and the mistakes made by lovers who are too slow in the uptake, and engage in self-questioning and doubt rather than take action when an opportunity presents itself. There would appear to be nothing historically or culturally Armenian in either the name of the heroine, or in the nature of her story. Gower is said to have taken the story from a medieval romance, the Lai du Trot, which was transmitted by the monk Helinand de Froidemont. Lines 1245–1504 consist of a story which begins thus:

> Of Armenie I rede thus,
> There was a king whiche Herupus
> Was hote, and he a lusty maide
> To doughter had, and as men saide
> Her name was Rosiphele,
> Which tho was of great renomee.
> For she was bothe wise and faire
> And shulde ben her faders heire.
> But she had o defaulte of Slouthe
> Towardes Love, and that was routhe.

The tale, in brief, tells of Rosiphele, who despite her beauty, was cold in love. One summer morning she took a walk in her delightful garden, through which a stream bubbled merrily, and, desiring to be alone, bade her maids withdraw. When she was by herself, there came through the woods 'a rout of ladies, in one livery'. These were all mounted on white steeds – save one who rode a black horse, in a sorry condition except for its fine bridle. The lady who rode upon it was ill-dressed, too. 'What is the meaning of this?' asked the Princess of Armenia. The lady replied that her companions were true servants of love, but she was being punished for her sloth in love: hence her degraded condition, in which she had been demoted from princess to ostler. But she had at least had one affair, and had received the bridle as a reward. In John Gower's poem, Rosiphele took note of her story, and resolved to mend her ways.[16]

At about this time the first recorded English (or supposedly English) traveller passed through Armenia. Sir John Mandeville – if he existed at all – probably wrote his *Travels* in 1356. (Some believe that his existence was just the product of the imagination of an inventive Normandy monk.) Assuming that he existed, he appears to have been, at different times, in the service of the Mamluk sultan of Egypt, and of the Great Khan of the Mongols; so he would have come across Armenians quite naturally. He tells us of the Castle of the Sparrowhawk, in Cilician Armenia, where the king met a lady of faery, with dire consequences; and he writes of men going from Trebizond 'to Ermonye the Great unto a cytee that is clept Artyroun [Erzerum], that was wont to ben a gode cytee and plenteous, but the Turkes han gretly wasted it'. He continues:

> Fro Artyroun go men to an Hille that is clept Sabisocolle. And there beside is another Hille that men clepen Ararathe: but the Jews clepen it Taneez, where Noes Schipp rested: and zit is upon that Montayne: and men may see it a ferr in cleer wedre: and that Montayne is well a 7 Myle high. And sum men seyn that they have seen and touched the Schipp; and put here Fyngres in the parties where the Feend went out whan that Noe seyd 'Benedicite'. But thei that seyn such wordes seyn here Willie, for a man may not gon up the Montayne for gret plentee of Snow that is alle weyes on that Mountayne nouther Somer ne Winter; so that no man may gon up there: ne nevere man did, sithe the tyme of Noe: saf a Monk that be the grace of God broughte on of the Plankes down, that zit is in the Mynstre at the foot of the Montayne. And besyde is the Cytee of Dayne that Noe founded. And faste by is the Cytee of Any, in the whiche were 1000 churches. But upon that Montayne to gon up this Monk had gret desir; and so upon a day he wente up and whan he was upward the 3 part of the Montayne he was so wery that he myghte no ferthere, and so he rested him and felle to slepe; and whan he awoke he fonde himself liggynge at the foot of the Montayne. And then he preyede devoutly to God that he wolde vouche saf to suffre him gon up. And an Angelle cam to him and seyde that he scholde gon up; and so he did. And sith that tyme never non. Wherfore men scholde not beleeve such Woordes.*[17]

---

\* From Erzerum men go to a hill that is called Sabisocoll. And there beside it is another called Ararat (but the Jews call it Taniz), where Noah's ship rested, and is upon that mountain. And men may see it from afar in clear weather. And that mountain is fully seven miles high. And some men say that they have seen and touched the ship, and put their fingers in the parts where the fiend went out when Noah said Benedicite. But they that say such words speak according to their own will; for a man may not go up the mountain for great plenty of snow that is always on that mountain – neither in summer nor winter, so that no man may go up there, nor ever did, since the time of Noah – save a monk that by the grace of God brought down one of the planks, that is in the monastery at the foot of the mountain. And beside is the city of Dvin that Noah founded. And fast by is the city of Ani, in which were 1000 churches. But this monk had a great desire to go up that mountain, and so one day he went up, and when he was about one third of the way up it, he was so weary that he could go no further, and so he rested and fell asleep; and when he awoke he found himself lying at the foot of the mountain. And then he prayed devoutly to God that he would vouchsafe to allow him to go up. And an angel came to him, and said he should go up; and so he did. And since that time never has anyone gone up. Wherefore men should not believe such words.

As the Middle Ages waned, the focus changed. With the end of Cilician Armenia, there could be no more direct diplomacy. But faith, and the memory of faith, would take Englishmen to Armenia. So too would commerce and adventure, as well as language, literature and scholarship. Ararat was an irresistible lure, whether for Noah's ark, for the unique thrill of the climb, or for the sheer luminous magnificence of its snow-clad peaks.

## CHAPTER 2

# 'A People Very Industrous in All Kind of Labour'
## John Cartwright and John Fryer

John Cartwright was the earliest English traveller we can be sure of who visited Armenia. Not much is known about him, apart from his name, his vocation of preacher, and that he had been a 'sometime student in Magdalen-College, in Oxford'. His book, *The Preacher's Travels*, was printed in 1611, and republished in the Harleian Collection of Voyages in 1745. Cartwright travelled extensively – 'to the Confines of the East Indies, through the great Countries of Syria, Mesopotamia, Armenia, Media, Hyrcania and Parthia', and returned 'by way of Persia, Susiana, Assyria, Chaldaea, and Arabia'. The date usually given for his journey is around 1593. This was an interesting time for Armenia. It was not many decades after the imposition of Ottoman rule on Western Armenia, and there was still a state of habitual war between the Ottoman sultan and the Persian shah. (Not until 1639 was a peace treaty drawn up between them.) In Armenia itself the country appeared to be recovering from the ravages of the Tamerlane and consequent disorders, and to be re-establishing some of its former traditional autonomy.

Cartwright also visited Armenia before Shah Abbas I of Persia's violent eviction in 1604 of large numbers of Armenians, whom he required to settle (principally) outside his new capital, Isfahan. Abbas I created a unique town for them, named New Julfa. The original Julfa was one of the principal cities in Armenia from which they were taken. Cartwright's account of old Julfa (which he spells 'Chiulfal') is interesting since it shows the prosperous civilization that the Armenians had created in their homeland by the late sixteenth century. Julfa is today outside Armenia; on present-day maps the town will be found in the Nakhichevan republic.

*A description of the people of Armenia, as they are at this day.*

At our first entrance into this country, we travelled through a goodly, large and spacious plain, compassed about with a row of high mountains, where

13

were many villages wholly inhabited by Armenians; a people very industrous
in all kind of labour: their women very skilful and active in shooting, and
managing any sort of weapon, like the fierce Amazons in ancient time;
and the women at this day, which inhabit the mountain at Xatach in
Persia. Their families are very great; for, both sons, nephews and nieces do
dwell under one roof, having all their substance in common: And when the
father dieth, the eldest son doth govern the rest; all submitting themselves
under his regiment. But when the eldest son dieth, the government doth
not pass to his sons, but to the eldest brother. And if it chance to fall out,
that all the brethren do die, then the government doth belong to the eldest
son of the eldest brother, and so from one to another. In their diet and
cloathing, they are all fed and cloathed alike, living in all peace and
tranquility, grounded on true love and honest simplicity.[1]

Cartwright remarks on the widely spread distribution of the Armenian
nation; and he notes 'their great liberty in the Ottoman kingdom'. This,
Cartwright avers, has been ascribed to their kings' high regard for
Mohammed during the lifetime of the prophet of Islam; but he believes
this to be the wrong explanation. The true reason is their commercial
acumen in Ottoman domains, and the benefit that the sultan has derived
from their skill. He mentions their two patriarchs (properly, catholicoses),
one at Sis, 'not far from Tharsus' and the other 'in the monastery of
Ecmeazin, near unto the city of Ervan in this country.' Eighteen monasteries, 'full fraught with friars of their religion; and four and twenty
bishopricks' are under them. Formerly the church was rich; but now, says
Cartwright, the sultan has seized the wealth, and the clergy 'are constrained to live on the alms of the people, going continually in visitation
from one city to another, carrying their wives and whole family with them.'

Their faith Cartwright berates for being 'spotted with superstitions',
but he offers the people a backhanded compliment in pointing out their
resistance to conversion to Rome.

They are (unless some few families) so far from yielding obedience unto the
see of Rome, that they assume all antiquity unto themselves, as having
retained the Christian faith from the time of the apostles. Many Jesuits and
priests have been sent from Rome to bring this oppressed nation under her
government, but they have little prevailed; for neither will they yield
obedience, nor will they be brought by any persuasion to forsake their
ancient and inveterate errors, to become more erroneous with her.

Having well refreshed ourselves among these villages, we proceeded in
our ordinary travel, but before we had passed two miles, certain troops of
Curdies encountered our caravan, with a purpose and intent to have robbed
the same, but finding themselves too weak to contend with such a company,
they departed until the next day following, when again they met us in a

very narrow passage between two mountains, where they made a stay of our whole caravan, exacting a shaughoe [shahi: a small coin] on every person which to purchase our peace we willingly paid.[2]

He travelled to Bitlis, about which he says little. His journey onwards to Van took three days; 'very wearisome'. He passed what he calls 'the lake Arctamar' and the 'Eckmenick islands, inhabited only by Armenians, and some Georgians, which two islands do bring forth and yield such store of cattle and plenty of rice, wheat and barley ... so these islands are to this day the garners and store-houses for all the country round about'.

Cartwright stayed five days in Van, which also receives little description, although he does point out that the city was formerly in the hands of the Persians, until it was conquered by the Turks. A digression on local geography leads to Mount Ararat.

The Turks call the mountain Gordaeus Augri-Daugh, the Armenians, Messis-saur: it is so high, that it over-tops all the mountains thereabouts. There issueth out of the foot of this hill a thousand little springs, wherof some do feed the river Tygris, and some other rivers; and it hath about it some three hundred villages inhabited by Armenians and Georgians; and also an ancient monastery dedicated to St Gregory, very large and spacious, able to receive Shaugh Tamas [Shah Tahmasp] the great king of Persia, and most of his army, who for the austere and strict life that he saw in those religious men, made him to spare it, and to change his determination, having a full purpose before to have destroyed it. About this monastery groweth great plenty of grain, the grain being twice as big as ours; as also roses and rhubarb, which, because they have not the skill to dry that simple, is of no esteem or value.[3]

As a preacher, Cartwright naturally gives his readers an uplifting account of Mount Ararat, the resting place of Noah's ark. Pieces of the ark, he was told by the friars, are still to be found at the top of the mountain; but the way up is guarded by angels, and anyone so bold as to venture up 'shall be brought down in the night season, from the place which he had gained in the daytime before'. Cartwright leaves this fable (which is very similar to that related by Sir John Mandeville) with its inventor, and repeats the scriptural version. He then travelled on, somewhat fearfully, to Julfa.

From the foot of this mountain, we spent a day's journey farther, towards Chiulfal; which day we travelled through very many narrow lanes in those mountains, and very deep valleys, wherein the river Araxis, with most outragious turnings and windings and his many rushing downfalls amongst the rocks doth even bedeaf a man's ears, and with his most violent roaming in and out, doth drown and overwhelm whosoever by miserable chance falleth down headlong from the top of those narrow passages which are upon the mountains. And upon the crests of the said mountains, on the side of the said narrow passages, there grew most hideous woods and antique forests, full of beeches, trees like poplars carrying mast fit for hogs, and pine-trees; where the horror of darkness, and silence which is often-times interrupted, only by the whistling winds, or by the cry of some wild beasts, do make the poor passengers most terribly afraid.

## The description of Chiulfal

At length our caravan ferry'd over the foresaid river and so we arrived at Chiulfal, a town situate on the frontiers between the Armenians and the Atropatians, and yet within Armenia, inhabited by Christians, partly Armenians, partly Georgians: a people rather given to the traffic of silks, and other sorts of wares, whereby it waxeth rich and full of money, than instructed in weapons and matters of war. This town consisteth of two thousand houses and ten thousand souls, being built at the foot of a great rocky mountain in so barren a soil, that they are constrained to fetch most of their provision, only wine excepted from the city Nassivan [Nakhich-evan], half a day's journey off, which some think to be Artaxata, in the confines of Media and Armenia. The buildings of Chiulfal are very fair, all of hard quarry stone; and the inhabitants very courteous and affable, great drinkers of wine, but no braulers in that drunken humour; and when they are most in drink, they pour out their prayers, especially to the Virgin Mary, as the absolute commander of her son Jesus Christ, and to other saints as intercessors. It is subject and tributary to the scepter of Persia, and contrarywise both by nature and affection great enemies to the Turk.[4]

Cartwright ends his description by relating an incident in which the inhabitants of Julfa were constrained to placate a Turkish pasha with 'a bountiful present', saying to him that of course, they would have given him their tribute voluntarily, except that it might have been misinterpreted by their Persian sovereign. No sooner had he departed with his gift than an emissary from the Persian shah arrived, and 'these poor Chiulfalini were glad to present the Persian prince with greater and more liberal gifts, than they did their enemy basha'. Here was a vivid example of the manner in which the people preserved their liberties and their lives.[5]

### JOHN FRYER

John Fryer's *New Account of East India and Persia, being Nine Years' Travels 1672–1681*, was published in 1688 and re-issued by the Hakluyt Society in 1912.

Fryer (who died in 1733) had studied at Trinity and Pembroke Colleges, Cambridge. He was a doctor, and he undertook his travels in the interests of the East India Company. His writing is lively, although his syntax is highly individual. After travelling to India, he entered Persia in February 1677. From Bandar Abbas, he went to Shiraz. He describes his entry into the latter city thus:

By break of day the Armenian Christians, which are numerous, came to congratulate our arrival, and brought banquets of wine, fruit, and a cold treat, with led horses of state, and loud musick, to make our entry the more pompous. In order whereunto, about eleven in the morning, conducted with much ceremony, we approached Siras, where we found spectators answerable to the novelty of our appearance, and the greatness of our train, with which we were passing through this city nigh two hours, before we were enclosed within the walls of the English house, which is a noble one, in the middle of a stately garden.[6]

Fryer emphasizes the skill of the Armenian traders: he points out their knowledge of trade, their honesty and their thrift on their journeys, spending fifty shillings (£2.50) 'where we cannot for fifty thomands': one thomand was equal to £3.33. He called them 'a kind of privateers in trade, no purchase, no pay'; they borrow from a benefactor – that is, their capital is borrowed from one of the houses of the Armenians of New Julfa – and on return 'a quarter part of the gain is their own: from such beginnings do they raise sometimes great fortunes for themselves and masters.'[7]

As regards the legal constitution of New Julfa, the Armenians appeared to be lightly governed. Their Persian governor ('one of the Suffean creed') only intervenes 'to put an end to those differences they cannot compose themselves.' Among themselves, they have

a civil magistrate of their own, elected yearly, to whose arbitriment, if they submit not, it is their own fault, nor can it be by any means imputed to the tyranny of the government, who leave them freely to try their own cases.

For so it was provided by Shaw Abas [Shah Abbas] when he deprived them of their own princes, and redeemed them from the Turkish slavery; between whose arms and the Persians, they hung miserably harassed, according to the successes of either's forces, for a long time; removing them from Erewan, Taberez and Syria, their native soil [Fryer's geography is a bit hazy here], he transplanted them to Jelfa, and shaded them under the protection of the queen mother, asserting thereby their rights and privileges in an higher manner (abating some little circumstances) than the Moors themselves; by which they became not only safe from their enemies, but they improved the glory of Spahaun [Isfahan] by their unwearied industry, there being many of them credible merchants at this time, accounted worth an hundred thousand thomand (each thomand being three pounds and a noble); so mightily do they increase under this umbrage, in riches and freedom; for whilst they sit lazily at home, their factors abroad in all parts of the earth return to their hives laden with honey; to which exercise, after they themselves have been brought up, they train their children under the safe conduct of experienced tutors, who instruct them first to labour for a livelihood, before they are permitted to expend.

Thus this prince not only expressed himself a good patron, but a prudent emperor, by favouring their designs, and taking all occasions from their adversaries of injuring them, exposed as they were to open violence; and at home securing them from the treachery and envy of his own subjects; not only allotting them a place over against his own palace to build their city, but encouraging them to rear costly and well-endowed temples, without any molestation, to the honour of the blessed name of Christ ...[8]

The majesty of the mother church at Jelfa rises not to that loftiness either to offend the eyes with its splendor, or to create a jealousy, from its prodigious structure, of another tower of Babel; but keeps the mean, as truly becomes the place separated for the service of the only True God; not so spacious as neat, leaning on four pillars, which bear an oval lanthorn, or crown, over the center of the dome, by which the chief lights are transmitted to the rest of the building, and by them the temple divided into four parts; the first whereof is almost all taken up by the high altar, garnished with images of the Blessed Mother and the Holy Child Jesus, unless a small ascent left for the singers, the bishop's chair, and for persons of quality among them; the side wings and the middle half way down the nave, being left for the men; all the rest is occupied by the women, even to the very folding doors of the temple. The roof or vault of the arches, the side walls and posts of the cathedral, are all painted with sacred histories.[9]

The outstanding passage in Fryer's account is his description of an Armenian wedding, as conducted in New Julfa. This is how he observed the ceremonies, by which the parties (as he puts it) 'commit matrimony'.

The eldest of the family on the husband's side opens the festival by first inviting the guests to the marriage feast, where the bridegroom appears in a mean dress and poorly habited, till the priests have received richer habiliments of the grandfathers, or eldest uncle's gift, and brought them covered into the middle of the guest-chamber, where they sanctify them and bless them for his use, the youth standing by; to verify what Paladius used for a proverb, *investem puerum quasi imberbem*, when he called a beardless boy by the epithet of an undressed lad; and every one taking their places, the servants lay them down on the carpets, and unwinding the silk embroidered for to wrap them in, discover only the bridegroom's suit, with an old rusty sword of the family's not worn since Shaw Abas reduced them; for in these countries it is not the custom that women of good fame, or repute, should meet in public conventions with the men, but they transact their own affairs in their own house of parliament among themselves.

On the heels of the servants come the clerks with their choir, and taking the cloaths, only one (which is all cloth of gold) being the uppermost garment is a loose coat of London cloth, without sleeves, lined with sables to keep off the winter's cold; when the reverend sages call forth the new married stripling, whom they place between two bridemen about his own age, they all three kneeling, while they sing the epithalamium, not so much as lifting up their heads till all the rites are finished; then they wait on the bridegroom in another room, whither his robes are carried, and when he is shifted, he returns attended by his bridemen; when every one of them salute the hands of all that are called to this solemnity, and, after an ancient custom, invite them to take a cold banquet among the tombs, to put them in mind of mortality at the same time they are contriving to continue the world.

The young spark being lift up on horseback, and some time carefully held by one on each side on foot, leads the way to the cavalcade, riding in state, after a noise of fidlers, drummers, pipers, and other lacquies, pages and footmen; after whom an innumerable concourse of horsemen follow to the graves (among whom are some very noble sepulchres fit to receive so great a company) but in fair weather they spread their carpets, and set up their tents near the side of a brook, almost washing their burial place.

Here Ceres and Bacchus having shewn their good will to Venus (for it is known without them no hearty sacrifice is paid to her) Hymen delivers out his torches, the sun having withdrawn his; and every one there takes a wax light in his hand, and mounting, direct themselves towards the city, in the same manner they came out, only bonfires, flambeaus, and fireworks illuminate the road all along: entring Jelfa, the stately gates of their friends and relations, especially such as are present at the collation, are bestuck with tapers in divers coloured paper lanthorns; which look gracefully and divert the company with variety of artful fires, each striving to outvie others; and are entertained at the same time with wine and sweetmeats, drinking of healths, and at last dismiss'd with fresh tapers given to all the guests.

This continues in the way to the cathedral, where about midnight the bridegroom arriving, begs the blessing of the archbishop, and they hardly return to the house from whence they set out, till almost break of day.

Where they are scarcely composed to sleep, before the father of the bride knocks on the same errand calling the guests to accept of a treat at his house; where those invited are carried into a noble open banquettinghouse in a garden, with tanks and adornments very magnificent, after their fashion; the room is perfumed with costly odours, smoking out of antick, weighty, silver perfuming pots, or pans; and being seated, voiders of sweetmeats (with Russian coat, as they call it) a dram of brandy is set before every one; and then the servants bring the best raiments yet presented the bridegroom, being the father-in-law's or his representatives; the ceremonies are the same of the clergy, only with this addition, the bridemen which kneeled yesterday, today stand upright with flaming flambeaus in their hands.

These ceremonies ended, and the sweetmeats taken off, a table is spread, and more than twice seven plates are differently modified to invite the palate to luxury ... here are such loads of provisions, that none need fear a quicker eye than appetite, at leisure to take notice what each eats; for should they do nothing but devour, their stomachs must be cloied before their portions sink.

Yet all these preparations with the enticing poinant sawces, and provoking pickles, prevail not on the bridegroom to fall to, till the father-in-law lays to his new son's double mess, a purse of gold; and this is the only thing they bear away by way of dowry: after this debt is cancelled, no cloud appears to disturb the mirth, eating, drinking, and facetious discourse is all the business; and in earnest it is one, and a tedious one where it lavishes into such excess ...

After shifting of plates unaccountably, and every one's health has reason done it, they take off the table-cloth, but not remove their seats; fruit, wine, tobacco, and salt bits for a whet, being placed before them, they continue drinking till midnight, being diverted by stage-players, dancers, and mountebanks all day; nor will they disdain to take up a tabor and roar out a song behind that, and a flute playing to them.

At night fireworks begin again, having had the constant ones of the water all the time, arising in crowns and garlands, with other figures; at last they bring the news that the matrons had dismissed the bride adorned with all her wealth and gallantry; when they rise, but proceed not till she is delivered to her groom, who waits on her to her horse; when they are both mounted, the ecclesiaticks marshal the procession; all the streets are illuminated, the loud drums and trumpets proclaim their approach; in the front is carried a tree full of fruit; after it follows the Europeans, then the Armenians in order; in the midst of them the canonical gentlemen and boys, singing and playing on musical instruments, all in their peculiar habits, which were rich, and the choiristers surplices full of red crosses; after these the bride and bridegroom, he nobly mounted and splendidly accoutred with magnificent trappings; his horse led, and the bride held on by matrons, cross-legg'd, after the country fashion for women to ride, but vailed all over with a saffron-coloured vail, lest if the blushes of the virgin bride should be discovered, or if too high a colour should be discerned in the maiden face, it may be imputed to the vail, not the floridness of the cheeks; after all, in the close of the procession, come the matrons attired in white sheets.

Nor do they go far before they repeat their banquets, with presents of tapers, sweetmeats, squibs, serpents and rockets, as they pass; the glory of this night is always designed to pay their respects to their governor in chief, who receives them very great, and grants a license for the youth to carry his spouse home, which he does, departing from hence to his father's house, where the company end their thalasses [festivities], and leave them to contemplate the joys of matrimony.[10]

## CHAPTER 3

# *'The Theatre of Perpetual War'*
# *Historians in the Eighteenth Century*

The greatest English historian of the eighteenth century, and perhaps of any century, was Edward Gibbon. His *History of the Decline and Fall of the Roman Empire* discourses with immense breadth and grandeur on the condition of Europe and Asia under the rule of the Second Rome, and naturally makes reference to Armenians.

However, besides Gibbon, there were in the same century other authors, much lesser figures, who make brief reference to the Armenians. One of these was Jonas Hanway (1712–86). In 1743 Hanway obtained a partnership in a trading house in St Petersburg, where he became a specialist in the Caspian trade. In 1750, having inherited a large sum of money, he abandoned international trade and came to London, where he devoted some of his time to philanthropy, but indulged much of it in pamphlet-eering and controversy. Dr Johnson said of him that he 'acquired some reputation by travelling abroad, but lost it all by travelling at home'. His two-volume work, *The Revolutions of Persia* (1753), is a chronicle rather than a history; it sets down details without much shape or style. It narrates the complex and disturbed history of Persia, Turkey and Russia in the late seventeenth and early eighteenth centuries.

At this time the Safavid dynasty of Persia was crumbling beneath the onslaught of the Afghans. In discussing the appearance of an Afghan force before the town of New Julfa, outside Isfahan, in 1722, Hanway gives his account of the foundation of that Armenian settlement. (The spelling of proper names has been modernized.)

> This town is situated a mile and a half south of Isfahan, on the south banks of the river Zainderud, on the side of which it is extended for almost three miles. It was founded by Abbas the Great, on the following occasion. The Armenians having revolted against the Turks, and submitted to this prince, he removed part of the inhabitants of Armenia into different provinces of Persia. Those of the ancient Julfa, a town on the banks of the Araxes, were transported to Isfahan, from whence they removed, and settled

in this place, to which they gave the name of their former residence. The people who had been drawn from Erivan, Shirvan, and the lower Armenia, settled in the suburbs of Isfahan; but Abbas, desirous of improving this new colony, obliged them to remove to Julfa, together with some Parsees of the neighbourhood of Kerman and Yezd; by this means, four new quarters were formed ... The Armenians being an industrious active people, applied themselves to commerce, and by their care and application this colony soon rose to a flourishing condition.

Abbas I was too great a politician to neglect any measure that might contribute to the welfare of such an establishment. He lent them considerable sums of money, without demanding any interest; he exempted them from all kinds of servitude; he granted them the free exercise of their religion; and in order to screen them from the jealousy and avarice of the Persian officers, he allowed them a Kalentar [chief magistrate] of their own nation, to whom he assigned a place at those celebrated feasts, in which, according to the custom of remotest antiquity, the kings of Persia dine in public with the grandees of the realm.

Some of the successors of this prince followed the same maxim, and Julfa in a very little time became a considerable place. It had the appearance of a republic, founded in the midst of a foreign nation; no Mohammedan was permitted to settle there, and the rigour of the law of retaliation [equal treatment for Armenians and Persians for murder], caused the inhabitants to be respected even by the Persians themselves. The Armenians of Julfa thus encouraged by so necessary a protection, were in a thriving condition for many years; and carried on, in different parts of the world, a considerable trade, which was very useful to the state. But at length the court, forgetful of its own interests, grew tired of favouring them; and in Shah Hussein's reign, their privileges, which had suffered some diminution under his predecessors fell into contempt. Under his government, no regard was paid to the law of retaliation. The [Muslim] ecclesiatics, offended at the equality which this law established between Mussulmans and Christians, introduced a custom, that if a Persian killed an Armenian, he should expiate the crime by giving a load of corn to the relations of the deceased. The Armenians considered this treatment as a mark of servitude: but they had no relief, and were equally a sport to the avarice of the great, and the insolence of the common people. While they groaned under these calamities, industry declined among them; the spirit of commerce, for which they had been so much distinguished, was in a great measure suppressed; and little more was thought of than to preserve their lives, and the property which they had already acquired.

The Armenians having thus been treated with contempt and injustice, it was feared they would cherish a resentment, which might induce them to change their masters. The Persians, tho' they now stood in need of their services, were jealous; and in this, as in many other instances, prepared the way to their own ruin, for fear of being undone. It ought naturally to have been expected that the Armenians, who are brave and tenacious of their property, would have struggled hard to be delivered from a rapacious enemy: however, upon the first news of [the Afghan] Maghmud's arrival, the king enjoined them to appear with their military equipage before his palace, intending, as he said, to entrust them with the guard of his person, during the absence of his household troops, who were going to march against the rebels. Flattered with this testimony of benevolence, they repaired to the place appointed in great numbers; but no sooner were they drawn up than they were commanded to lay down their arms and dismissed with strict orders to deliver up what arms might still be remaining among them ...

Things were thus situated, when the Afghans appeared before Julfa: they attacked the place the very night they arrived, and the assault lasted two hours. In order to make the enemy believe they had regular troops, the Armenians, during the engagement, called each other by Persian names; and tho' they were very indifferently armed, yet they defended themselves with so much bravery, that the utmost the enemy could do was to seize a little entrenchment, which had been thrown up in a hurry ...[1]

The Armenians were at length compelled to surrender to the Afghans, who demanded as indemnity 70,000 tomans (£175,000), and, much more galling, 'a certain number of young virgins'.

The Armenians are jealous to the highest degree of their honour, so that nothing could cut them deeper than to deliver up their daughters. The disconsolate mothers made Julfa resound with their lamentations. Some of those young maids were so shocked to see themselves abandoned to the enemies of their country, that they died with excessive grief. The Afghans, whose hearts could not but feel, in some measure, the distress of these young women, and whose religion by no means allows of any violence, sent those home who were most afflicted; and others were ransomed by their parents; insomuch that in a few days, there remained but a small part of them in slavery.[2]

By this time, when the Safavid dynasty was collapsing, the Armenians of Mountainous Karabagh, at the eastern edge of the Armenian homeland, had maintained a kind of semi-independence for 300 years – ever since their autonomy, backed up by standing armies created from their own people, had been confirmed by Jahan Shah of the Black Sheep Turkoman confederation. In the disturbed times of the 1720s their armies were compelled to take to the field to protect this autonomy. Further south, the Armenians of Siunik were being welded into a nation by an Armenian from Tiflis, David Bek, who for a dozen years created conditions of empire-free autonomy, showing military competence by defeating a Turkish army at Halidsor. Hanway, describing events of 1726, relates the following, which is interesting in that it shows Armenians again victorious over a Turkish force:

> The winter had passed without any action worth notice, except that of Savi Mustafa, who marched out of Ganja of which he was governor, and dispersed the Armenians of Shamakhie. These people taking advantage of the present circumstances, formed themselves into a kind of republic, which, as we have mentioned [Hanway is mistaken here; there is no earlier mention], distinguished itself by the total defeat of a body of six thousand men, whom Abdallah Basha had sent against them the preceding summer. It was not long before they had their revenge also of the governor of Ganja. It was their custom to assemble in great numbers during Easter, in a plain in that neighbourhood. Having received intelligence that the Turks had formed a design to surprize them on this occasion, they took their measures, and not only defended themselves, but also drew the Turks into their defiles, where they obtained an easy victory over them.[3]

The genius of the century, however, in comparison to whom others are chroniclers, was Edward Gibbon. His great work, first published in 1776, has long been applauded as a masterpiece of scholarship and literary style, showing a magnificent grasp of diverse sources. Where it parts company with modern historical values is that to some extent it is an ideological history, making a point about 'decline', and demonstrating the qualities and the perceptions (and maybe the prejudices) of the author's century, in a way similar to those of the following century, where we find hidden axioms concerning inevitable progress. Nevertheless one can read the work and relish the occasional prejudice, and at the same time allow oneself to be dazzled by the marvellous narrative, superbly controlled for the reader, and to be struck by an arresting idea.

In his account of the disputes between Rome and Persia, Gibbon naturally makes a number of references to Armenians. Two other passages are especially worth recording; one on the origins of the faith in Armenia, and the other a daring hypothesis on the legacy of Armenian religious dissent to western Europe. As regards the origin of Christianity in Armenia, it is a minor matter of regret that Gibbon misunderstands the Armenian theological position: he calls the Armenians 'pure disciples of Eutyches', that is, followers of the theology of a man who was an extreme monophysite, even though in the Armenian liturgy the name of Eutyches is anathematized as that of a heretic. (In the extract, the theological passages have been omitted). Gibbon also underestimates the learning and literature of Armenia – he seems unaware of the writings of the Armenian church fathers – and he passes by the artistic achievements shown in Armenian churches and manuscripts. Maybe these aspects of the

Armenian nation were unknown to Europeans at that time. His narrative makes the people out to be more helpless than they actually were. On the subject of the Armenian monarchy, it is also unfortunate that he neglects the Bagratid kings (886–1064), with their capital at Ani, who achieved great things for the Armenian people.

Since the age of Constantine, the Armenians had signalized their attachment to the religion and empire of the Christians. The disorders of their country, and their ignorance of the Greek tongue, prevented their clergy from assisting at the synod of Chalcedon, and they floated 84 years in a state of indifference or suspense ... The religion of Armenia could not derive much glory from the learning or the power of its inhabitants. The royalty expired with the origin of their schism; and their Christian kings, who arose and fell in the thirteenth century on the confines of Cilicia, were the clients of the Latins and the vassals of the Turkish sultan of Iconium. The helpless nation has seldom been permitted to enjoy the tranquillity of servitude. From the earliest period to the present hour, Armenia has been the theatre of perpetual war: the lands between Tauris [Tabriz] and Erivan were dispeopled by the cruel policy of the Sophis [Persians]; and myriads of Christian families were transplanted, to perish or to propagate in the distant provinces of Persia. Under the rod of oppression, the zeal of the Armenians is fervent and intrepid; they have often preferred the crown of martyrdom to the white turban of Mohammed; they devoutly hate the error and idolatry of the Greeks; and their transient union with the Latins is not less devoid of truth than the thousand bishops whom their patriarch offered at the feet of the Roman pontiff.

The *catholic* [catholicos], or patriarch, of the Armenians resides in the monastery of Ekmiasin, three leagues from Erivan. Forty-seven archbishops, each of whom may claim the obedience of four or five suffragans, are consecrated by his hand; but the far greater part are only titular prelates, who dignify with their presence and service the simplicity of his court. As soon as they have performed the liturgy, they cultivate the garden; and our bishops will hear with surprise that the austerity of their life increases in just proportion to the elevation of their rank. In the fourscore thousand towns or villages of his spiritual empire, the patriarch receives a small and voluntary tax from each person above the age of fifteen; but the annual amount of six hundred crowns is insufficient to supply the incessant demands of charity and tribute. Since the beginning of the last century the Armenians have obtained a large and lucrative share of the commerce of the east; in their return from Europe, the caravan usually halts in the neighbourhood of Erivan, the altars are enriched with the labours of their patient industry; and the faith of Eutyches is preached in their recent congregations of Barbary and Poland.[4]

On the subject of the heterodox Paulicians, Gibbon makes some daring surmises, indicative of his bold and speculative outlook. The Paulicians were an early Protestant community of believers who emerged in the ninth century. They believed in taking the gospels and epistles at face value, and in dispensing with the Old Testament, most of the sacraments, and the church hierarchy. They also had no time for the cults of saints and the Virgin Mary. Theologically, they inclined to dualism. A modern specialist on the sect, Professor Nina Garsoian, has said that there is 'little doubt that Paulicianism originally developed in Armenia'. She further says that 'by its later stages, Paulicianism was spread from Syria, across Armenia and Asia Minor, possibly to Crete, eventually to Italy, and unquestionably to the Balkans.' The movement was widely spread and deeply rooted.

Gibbon spends all of chapter 54 of his great work in describing the origin, nature and consequences of the Paulician reformation. This chapter made a deep impression on F. C. Conybeare, the pioneer of Armenian scholarship in Britain. The historian shows considerable favour towards this community, and vividly describes the fortification of its city at Tephrice (modern Divrig, Turkey), and the defeats its people inflicted on the Byzantine army. He continues:

About the middle of the eighth century, Constantine [V], surnamed Copronymus by the worshippers of images, had made an expedition into Armenia, and found, in the cities of Melitene and Theodosiopolis [Malatya and Erzerum], a great number of Paulicians, his kindred heretics. As a favour, or punishment, he transplanted them from the banks of the Euphrates to Constantinople and Thrace; and by this emigration their doctrine was introduced and diffused in Europe. If the sectaries of the metropolis were soon mingled with the promiscuous mass, those of the country struck a deep root in a foreign soil. The Paulicians of Thrace resisted the storms of persecution, maintained a secret correspondence with their Armenian brethren, and gave aid and comfort to their preachers, who solicited, not without success, the infant faith of the Bulgarians ... Their exile in a distant land was softened by a free toleration: the Paulicians held the city of Philippopolis [Plovdiv] and the keys of Thrace; the Catholics were their subjects; the Jacobite emigrants their associates: they occupied a line of villages and castles in Macedonia and Epirus; and many native Bulgarians were associated to the communion of arms and heresy.[5]

Gibbon then discourses upon the temporary victory of Alexius Comnenus over the Paulicians of Thrace, and notes their revival upon the death of Comnenus. He continues:

Three different roads might introduce the Paulicians into the heart of Europe. After the conversion of Hungary the pilgrims who visited Jerusalem might safely follow the course of the Danube: in their journey and return they passed through Philippopolis; and the sectaries, disguising their name and heresy, might accompany the French or German caravans to their respective countries. The trade and dominion of Venice pervaded the coast of the Adriatic, and the hospitable republic opened her bosom to foreigners of every climate and religion. Under the Byzantine standard the Paulicians were often transported to the Greek provinces of Italy and Sicily: in peace and war they freely conversed with strangers and natives, and their opinions were silently propagated in Rome, Milan, and the kingdoms beyond the Alps.

It was in the country of the Albigeois, in the southern provinces of France, that the Paulicians were most deeply implanted; and the same vicissitudes of martyrdom and revenge which had been displayed in the neighbourhood of the Euphrates were repeated in the thirteenth century on the banks of the Rhone. The laws of the Eastern Emperors were revived by Frederic the Second. The insurgents of Tephrice were represented by the barons and cities of Languedoc: Pope Innocent III surpassed the sanguinary fame of Theodora ... The visible assemblies of the Paulicians, or Albigeois, were extirpated by fire and sword; and the bleeding remnant escaped by flight, concealment, or Catholic conformity. But the invincible spirit which they had kindled still lived and breathed in the western world. In the state, in the church, and even in the cloister, a latent succession was preserved by the disciples of St Paul, who protested against the tyranny of Rome, embraced the bible as a rule of faith, and purified their creed from all the visions of the Gnostic theology. The struggles of Wickliff in England, of Huss in Bohemia, were premature and ineffectual; but the names of Zuinglius, Luther, and Calvin are pronounced with gratitude as the deliverers of nations.[6]

## CHAPTER 4

# 'It Was in Armenia that Paradise was Placed'
# Byron in Venice

From the Middle Ages to the early nineteenth century, few contacts were made with Armenia except by missionaries (who became linguists and even scholars), or those with a business link, such as John Fryer or Jonas Hanway. The age of travel for its own sake, and of pleasure-in-ruins, lay dormant; and even when it awoke, Armenia was far from the paths of the Grand Tour. In English literature there appears to have been no reference to Armenians between Gower and Byron. No individual Armenian appears, or is even referred to, in Marlowe's Malta, or in *Othello*, which is, of Shakespeare's plays, the one where we would most likely meet an Armenian, perhaps illuminating the Moor's memories of his time in Aleppo; although it is worth noting that Enobarbus' superb Act II speech in *Antony and Cleopatra*, 'The barge she sat in, like a burnish'd throne, Burn'd on the water ...' is a close re-working of a passage from Plutarch's Lives, in which the author describes Cleopatra's progress down the River Cydnus, situated in Cilician Armenia.

Byron was the extraordinary luminary whose interest in Armenians briefly shone in 1816–17. The poet never ceases to amaze with his individuality, his joyous and sensuous poetical genius and his astonishing ability to fuse the personal and universal (for surely 'political' is too narrow a word for his hatred of oppression). His intense response to the past history and present condition of foreign lands, and his sublime conscious-ness of landscape, revolutionized not only the entire temper of poetry, but also brought into literary discourse subjects which had not hitherto been considered suitable to it. Literature lived, moved and mattered, as much as the relentless march of armies, the implacable decisions of tyrants, and the unquiet rebellion of the people. Byron's thrilling sensibility meant that poetry became part of life, and life of poetry. *Childe Harold* and *Don Juan* are at once deeply personal and astonishingly public, ranging over history, politics, landscape, love, light and art.

Elsewhere in the arts, especially in painting and music, romanticism

29

was bringing the political into the area of creativity: one thinks of the canvases of Jacques-Louis David, or of Goethe's and Beethoven's *Egmont*. The new conceptions of art drew much of their sustenance from the ideas of the French Revolution, especially from the notion that the liberty of the individual counted (rather than say the survival of some declining but still tyrannical dynasty such as that of the Sicilian Bourbons, or the continuation of some antique politico–religious ideology). Liberty was held to be a highly prized quality, and was thus among the central subjects of art.

Byron was of course dedicated to the struggle for the freedom for Greece in his last years. The story of the humane and fallible manner in which he carried on this struggle, fighting against his own inertia, and against the divisions among the various groups struggling for independence, is a profound tale of the ambiguities and ironies of true commitment. (One of the ironies of the situation is that Byron held a genuine regard for Ali Pasha, the tyrant of Epirus.) But at the time of the poet's interest in Armenians, the struggle for Greece was still in the future. Even that for Italy, which was to burn brightly when the charms of Teresa Guiccioli touched his heart, was not yet defined. While studying Armenian his hard work was softened by the enchantments of Marianna Segati, the wife of his landlord.

Nevertheless it is perhaps worthwhile to note a couple of Byron's observations on the Hellenic situation and the prospects for liberty there. In 1811 he wrote that 'while every man of any pretensions to learning is tiring out his youth, and often his age, in the study of the language and of the harangues of the Athenian demagogues in favour of freedom, the real or supposed descendants of these sturdy republicans are left to the actual tyranny of their masters, although a very slight effort is required to strike off their chains'.[1]

Despite this ironical look at schooldays, and despite his own poetic idealism, Byron was in practical terms no extremist or wild builder of extravagant schemes for the Greeks or against the Turks. He held no illusions about the tyrannical nature of Ottoman government. But he criticized those with too great a zeal for the Greeks:

> Eton and Sonnini [that is, William Eton and Sonnini de Manoncourt, two ardent philhellenes] have led us astray by their panegyrics and projects; but, on the other hand, De Pauw and Thornton [that is, Cornelius de Pauw and Thomas Thornton, author of *The Present State of Turkey*, 1807] have debased the Greeks beyond their demerits.[2]

The poet who stunned the reading public with *Childe Harold's Pilgrimage* in 1812, and who held such an profound passion for freedom, might be a friend of individual Turks such as Ali Pasha, but could not ever be a friend of Ottoman Turkey. Ardour on behalf of the Turks' empire was for manufacturers, military strategists, admirers of the implacable, and devotees of imperial power. For Byron, other sentiments were uppermost:

> Spirit of Freedom! when on Phyle's brow
> Thou satst with Thrasubulus and his train
> Couldst thou forbode the dismal hour which now
> Dims the green beauties of thine Attic plain?
> Not thirty tyrants now enforce the chain,
> But every carle can lord it o'er thy land;
> Nor rise thy sons, but idly rail in vain,
> Trembling beneath the scourge of Turkish hand,
> From birth to death enslaved; in word, in deed, unmanned.[3]

> ... know ye not
> Who would be free themselves must strike the blow
> By their right arms the conquest must be wrought
> Will Gaul or Muscovite redress ye? No![4]

Byron arrived in Venice in 1816, and took up the study of the Armenian language, feeling that he needed something 'craggy' to break his mind on. (His emotions were focused on the figure of Marianna Segati.) He actually studied two Armenian languages. One was that used for everyday speaking and writing, which is in use today amongst the Armenian community world-wide. The other was the ancient, heavily inflected tongue, the language of the Armenian bible and liturgy, which today is spoken only in church. Byron sought mastery of both.

He studied them under the guidance of Father Pasquale Aucher (in Armenian, Avgerian or Augerian) at the Armenian monastery of San Lazzaro, which still exists in the Venice lagoon. The monks of this order are known as Mekhitarists, named after Mekhitar of Sebastia (or Sivas), who had founded the order, initially in Constantinople, in 1701. One part of the brotherhood had moved to San Lazzaro in 1717.

To John Murray, Byron wrote (4 December 1816):

I wrote to you at some length last week, so that I have little to add, except that I had begun, and am proceeding in a study of the Armenian language, which I acquire as well as I can, at the Armenian convent, where I go every day to take lessons of a learned friar, and have gained some singular and not useless information with regard to the literature and customs of that oriental people. They have an establishment here – a church and convent of seventy monks, very learned and accomplished men, some of them. They also have a press, and make great efforts for the enlightening of their nation. I find the language, (which is twin, the literal and the vulgar) difficult, but not invincible (at least I hope not). I shall go on. I found it necessary to twist my mind round some severer study, and this, as being the hardest I could devise here, will be a file for the serpent.[5]

Byron wrote to Thomas Moore (5 December 1816):

By way of divertisement, I am studying daily, at an Armenian monastery, the Armenian language. I found that my mind wanted something craggy to break upon; and this – as the most difficult thing I could discover here for an amusement – I have chosen, to torture me into attention. It is a rich language, however, and would amply repay any one the trouble of learning it. I try, and shall go on; – but I answer for nothing, least of all for my intentions or my success. There are some very curious MSS. in the monastery, as well as books; translations also from Greek originals, now lost, and from Persian and Syriac &c.; besides works of their own people. Four years ago the French instituted an Armenian professorship. Twenty pupils presented themselves on Monday morning, full of noble ardour, ingenuous youth, and impregnable industry. They persevered, with a courage worthy of the nation and of universal conquest, until Thursday; when fifteen of the twenty succumbed to the six-and-twentieth letter of the alphabet. It is, to be sure, a Waterloo of an alphabet – that must be said for them.[6]

Byron evidently worked hard with Father Pasquale on his Armenian grammar. On 27 December 1816 he wrote to Murray:

I am going on with my Armenian studies in a morning, and assisting and stimulating in the English portion of an English and Armenian grammar now publishing at the Convent of St Lazarus. The Superior of the Friars is a bishop and a fine old fellow, with the beard of a meteor. My spiritual preceptor, pastor and master, Father Paschal, is also a learned and pious soul – he was two years in England.[7]

A few days later (2 January 1817), he wrote to Murray:

In another sheet I send you some sheets of a grammar, English and Armenian, for the use of the Armenians, of which I promoted and indeed induced the publication (it cost me but a thousand francs of French livres). I still pursue my lessons in the language, without any rapid progress, but advancing a little daily. Padre Paschal, with some little help from me as a translator of his Italian into English, is also proceeding in an MS grammar for the English acquisition of Armenian, which will be printed also when written. We want to know if there are any *Armenian types* or letterpress in England, at Oxford, Cambridge or elsewhere? You know I suppose that many years ago the two Whistons published in England an original text of a history of Armenia with their own Latin translation.* Do these types still exist? & where. Pray enquire among your learned acquaintance. When this grammar (I mean the one now printing) is done, will you have any objection to take 40 or 50 copies which will not cost in all above five or ten guineas, and try the curiosity of the learned with the sale of them. Say yes or no as you like. I can assure you that they have some very curious books and MS, chiefly translations from Greek originals now lost. They are besides a much respected and learned community, and the study of their language was taken up with great ardour by some literary Frenchmen in Buonaparte's time.[8]

At about this time he wrote a preface intended for the Armenian grammar but which was not used since Father Pasquale objected to its anti-Turkish tone. For us, it is hard to see why. Byron wrote of the 'neatness, the comfort, the gentleness, the unaffected devotion, the accomplishments, and the virtues of the brethren of the order' – men who 'are the priesthood of an oppressed and noble nation'. On the political and social condition of the nation, Byron said:

... they have long occupied, nevertheless, a part of the House of Bondage, who has lately multiplied her many mansions. It would be difficult, perhaps, to find the annals of a nation less stained with crimes than those of the Armenians, whose virtues have been those of peace, and their vices those of compulsion. But whatever may have been their destiny – and it has been bitter – whatever it may be in the future their country must ever be one of the most interesting in the globe; and perhaps their language only requires to be more studied to become more attractive. If the Scriptures are rightly understood, it was in Armenia that Paradise was placed – Armenia, which has paid as dearly as the descendants of Adam for that fleeting participation of its soil in the happiness of him who was created from its dust. It was in Armenia that the flood first abated, and the dove alighted. But with the disappearance of Paradise itself may be dated almost the unhappiness of the country; for though long a powerful kingdom, it was scarcely ever an independent one, and the satraps of Persia and the pachas of Turkey have alike desolated the region where God created man in his own image.[9]

One of Byron's 'Detached Thoughts', a series of dazzling random reflections which he jotted down between October 1821 and May 1822,

---

* William Whiston was a Cambridge professor who lost his post on account of his Newtonian views. One of his sons John was a Fleet Street bookseller. Two other sons, George and William published an edition of Movses Khorenatsi's *History of the Armenians* in 1736, with an Armenian typeface cut for the purpose by William Caslon. The Armenian text is printed alongside a Latin translation.

shows the impact of the study of the Armenian language on his brilliant, mercurial temperament:

> I set in zealously for the Armenian and Arabic – but I fell in love with some absurd womankind both times before I had overcome the Characters and at Malta & Venice left the profitable Orientalists for – for – (no matter what – ) notwithstanding that my master the Padre Pasquale Aucher (for whom by the way I compiled the major part of two Armenian & English grammars) assured me 'that the terrestrial Paradise had been certainly in Armenia' – I went seeking it – God knows where – did I find it? – Umph! – Now & then – for a minute or two.[10]

With the assistance of Father Pasquale, Byron also translated some New Testament texts which exist in the Armenian but not in the Greek. He wrote of his labour to Thomas Moore (31 March 1817): 'Did I tell you that I have translated two Epistles? A correspondence between St Paul and the Corinthians, not to be found in our version, but the Armenian, but which seems to me to be very orthodox, and I have done it into scriptural prose.'[11] Here is part of the text:

> But you also, Corinthians! have known from the seeds of wheat, and from other seeds;
> That one grain falls dry into the earth, and within it first dies;
> And afterwards rises again by the will of the Lord indued with the same body:
> Neither indeed does it arise the same simple body, but manifold, and filled with blessing.
> But we must produce the example not only from seed but from the honorable bodies of men.
> Ye have also known Jonas the son of Amittai;
> Because he delayed to preach to the Ninevites, he was swallowed up in the belly of a fish for three days and three nights:
> And after three days God heard his supplication, and brought him out from the deep abyss;
> Neither was any part of his body corrupted, neither was his eyebrow bent down;
> And how much more for you, oh men of little faith!
> If you believe in our Lord Jesus Christ, he will raise you up, even as he himself has risen.
> If the bones of Elisha the prophet falling upon the dead, revived the dead,
> By how much more shall ye, who are supported by the flesh and the blood and the Spirit of Christ, arise again on that day, with a perfect body?

Byron also translated an extract from a Synodical Discourse by Nerses of Lambron (1153–98), one of the architects of the kingdom of Cilicia, and a temporal and spiritual adviser to Prince (later King) Levon II.

> It was beautiful then to behold Christ as a bridegroom nobly adorned for the nuptial chamber, who spake with a soft voice to his most pure beloved: 'Enlarge the place of thy tent, and of thy porch; spare not, plant it, lengthen thy cords, and strengthen thy stakes; for thou shalt break forth on the right hand and on the left, and thy seed shall inherit the gentiles, and thou shalt renew the ruined cities of the idolaters. Fear not, though till now by means of these I have covered thee with confusion. For I swear, that I shall never repent to make my abode of pleasure with thee who art my repose for ever and ever.'
>
> Then the first enemy, in ambush for his prey, perceiving that his snares were discovered, and that the worship of God flourished throughout the world, observing that those who had been deceived were redeemed, and that the inheritors of paradise returned to their country, that the celestial holiness poured forth its glory, that the instrument of hatred being broken, the fruits of charity began to multiply themselves, and the hope of all no longer turned to the earth, ascended to the heavenly abodes. Forth from the cave of his malice he issued, like the lion roaring in his anger, and roamed about with open and insatiate jaws, to devour the church recovered by Christ.[12]

Byron cannot really be credited with making any section of the British people aware of the Armenians and their history, language and culture. His personal enthusiasm for them is evident from his letters, but it does not appear to have been shared by his correspondents. His study of their history and language remained largely in the domain of grammarians and antiquaries – although the Armenian grammar was popular, reprinting in 1819, 1832, and 1873. But in the wider public domain, what he did for the succeeding generations of Armenians and their supporters was to open the door in Europe to the idea of ending serfdom in the east, especially for the non-Turkish peoples of the Ottoman empire, hitherto religious flocks and now becoming national communities. He gave a western articulation to the aspirations of the Greeks, and by extension to those of other Ottoman nationalities. He showed that they were real people with real aspirations. As a result of Byron's brilliant and ironical love of liberty, and his value of the individual in an age dominated by despotic imperial collectivism, their oppression began to be understood. The members of the communities came to be seen as people whose individual liberty mattered, when hitherto they had been perceived as mere cogs in some antique imperial system, or as half-forgotten relics exotic in their medievalness.

## CHAPTER 5

# 'A Vast Solitude on the Grey and Wintry Plain'
## Sir Robert Ker Porter, Richard Wilbraham
## and James Brant

In the nineteenth century, the British were among the most intrepid travellers to Armenia. (At the time, of course, conditions were much like as had been at the time of Cartwright's travels; there were no roads, no transport, and almost nowhere for visitors to stay.) Some went out of natural curiosity; some may have been on intelligence missions, since the region was, in terms of strategic geography, a sensitive area; there were scientists, historians, geographers, missionaries and mountaineers. Their writings constitute an important and interesting record.

Most of them travelled via Constantinople, the Black Sea and Trebizond, but a number also approached Armenia through the east. Here we find men in the Indian or Persian service. They were un-encumbered with prejudices (either for or against) on the subject of Ottoman Turkish rule; and they could open-mindedly compare the state of affairs in eastern Armenia, which was first Persian, then Russian, with that in western or Turkish Armenia.

### SIR ROBERT KER PORTER

Sir Robert Ker Porter (1777–1842) was an artist, soldier, author and diplomat. In 1805–7 he travelled in northern Russia and Sweden; and returned in 1817 for extensive travels in southern Russia and Persia. At this time Georgia had recently been incorporated into the Russian empire, and present-day Armenia lay in the domains of Persia. (However the mountainous region of Karabagh, had been conquered by Russia in 1805.) He published an account of his later travels in a major two-volume work, *Travels in Georgia, Persia, Armenia and Ancient Babylon* (1821). Here is his account of visiting the ruins of Ani, the Armenian medieval capital city, at present just inside Turkey, on the very frontier with Armenia. H. F. B. Lynch, writing in the 1890s, ridicules this passage as a 'fantastic description', but it might possibly have been more accurate than Lynch's abrupt dismissal indicates. Ker Porter's writing has a magnificent cold grandeur to it, and conveys marvellously a sense of the consolation of art and history in the course of a harsh Asiatic journey.

My escort told me we had then about ten versts [6²/₃ miles] before we should arrive at Ani. The day was far advanced, and being eager to reach the place time enough to allow some hours of examination, we set off at a very rapid pace. The road was exceedingly rough, over low hills, where often a track was scarcely visible; but at length the towers of the ancient city appeared at the extremity of an uneven plain, spreading to a vast extent along the horizon. Impatient, I spurred on; and, at a nearer view, found its southern and eastern faces protected by a deep and impassable ravine, through which passes the Arpa Chai.

The western and northern fronts have been defended by a double range of high walls and towers of the finest masonry. Three great entrances present themselves to the north. Over the centre gate was sculptured a leopard or lion-passant; and near it, on the flanking towers, several large crosses were carved in the stone, and richly decorated with exquisite fretwork.

On entering the city, I found the whole surface of the ground covered with hewn stones, broken capitals, columns, shattered but highly ornamented friezes; and other remains of ancient magnificence. Several churches, still existing in different parts of the place, retain something more than ruins of their former dignity; but they are as solitary as all the other structures, on which time and devastation have left more heavy strokes.

In the western extremity of this great town, in which no living beings, except ourselves, seemed breathing, we saw the palace, once of the kings of Armenia; and it is a building worthy the fame of this old capital. Its length stretches nearly the whole breadth, between the walls of the city on the one side, and the ravine on the other. Indeed, it seems a town in itself; and so superbly decorated within and without, that no description can give an adequate idea of the richness of the highly wrought carvings on the stone, which are all over the building; or of the finely executed mosaic patterns, which beautify the floors of its countless halls.

Near the centre of the city, rise two enormous octagon towers of an immense height, surmounted by turrets. They command all around them, even to the citadel, which stands to the south west on a high rock, and at the edge of a precipice. The farther I went, and the closer I examined the remains of this vast capital, the greater was my admiration for its firm and finished masonry.

In short, the masterly workmanship of the capitals of the pillars, the nice carvings of the intricate ornaments and arabesque friezes, surpassed anything of the kind I had ever seen, whether abroad, or in the most celebrated cathedrals of England. I particularly observed a religious edifice, of less dimensions than some of the others, but of exquisite architecture. It stood very near the octagon towers; and its high arched roof was a beautiful specimen of mosaic work, enriched with borders of the pure Etruscan, formed in red, black and yellow stone. The pillars, and all ornamental parts of the building were as sharp and fresh, as if but the erection of yesterday.

Indeed everywhere time seemed to have dealt more mercifully with this city, than the hand of man. War had broken down its bulwarks; made its palaces, churches and dwelling-places tenantless; and in a thousand ways left its desolating marks. But where time alone might be expected to act, or with its destroying auxiliaries, the influences of weather, there we found few symptoms of decay. Fine and even brilliant mosaic, executed with more or less precision, spreads itself over the city; and in general the form of the cross seems to be the root whence all the various patterns spring. Houses, churches, towers, embattled walls, every structure high or low, partake the prevailing taste; and on all we see the holy insignia carved, large or small, in black stone.

Besides these emblems, I found long inscriptions, cut in the old Armenian character, over the principal entrances of the churches; and some of them I should have transmitted to paper, had not the evening been drawing on, and with it a cold so intense as to disable me from holding my pencil. But, had it been otherwise, the impatience of my escort to be gone would not have allowed me to trace a line. Notwithstanding their numbers, and their courage, it was probable that, under dusk, they might be surprised by a greater force, of equal determination – banditti, issuing from the dark and tomb-like heaps of the city, where, in the daylight, appeared only silence and desolation. The disposition of many of the ruins, by their closeness and gloom, rendered them apt places for the lurking-holes of these sanguinary freebooters; like most Asiatic cities, the streets appearing to have been not more than from twelve to fourteen feet wide. The generality of the houses along these narrow but widely scattered lines were divided into a variety of small apartments, which are easily traced in the divisions of the roofless walls.

As I passed by them, and over the almost formless masses of yet more extensive ruins, I could not but think of the interesting stores of antiquity which might be lying hid beneath those mighty fragments of columns, walls and heaps of stones. Even a few days' gathering on the surface would furnish a traveller (could it be attempted with any security) with very fine specimens of the most beautiful ornaments of architecture. The military power of the city, as far as fortifications could render it formidable, must have been very great; for the ravine which I mentioned before, as one means of defence, was additionally strengthened with walls and towers of different heights. The remains of a noble stone bridge are yet visible over the river which flows at the bottom of the ravine. When the sun had quite sunk behind the mountains, it was no time to linger longer in such a place; and with infinite regret I obeyed the summons of my guides, and took a last look of the majestic relics of Ani, lying, a vast solitude, on the grey and wintry plain.[1]

### CAPTAIN RICHARD WILBRAHAM

About twenty years later the site of Ani was visited by Captain Richard Wilbraham of the 7th Royal Fusiliers, 'lately employed on a particular service in Persia'. John Murray published his account of his travels in 1839. It is interesting that he too mentions the palace of the kings of Armenia, an edifice that had disappeared by the time of later visitors. Maybe Ker Porter had not been so fanciful. The fate of the palace of Ani must remain one of the many intriguing puzzles associated with Armenia's past. Wilbraham describes his visit to the former Armenian capital thus:

The massive towers and churches appear in perfect preservation; and the long line of wall which crowns the rocky heights masks the ruin which prevails within. The site of Ani has been most judiciously selected with a view to strength. The southern face is protected by a deep and precipitous ravine, at the bottom of which flows the rapid stream of the Arpa Chai, here no longer fordable. Two other faces terminate in rocky and abrupt declivities; and the third, which alone is open to attack, is defended by a wall of massive masonry flanked by numerous towers.

We entered by the principal gate, which stands in the centre of this face. Over the gateway are some curiously sculptured figures. The walls and towers are built of irregular masses of stone, cemented with mortar, but they are faced with well-hewn blocks of sandstone. The sacred symbol of Christianity is introduced in various places. Huge blocks of blood-red stone, let into the masonry of the tower, form gigantic crosses, which have defied the hand of the destroying Moslem.

The only buildings which are now standing are the Christian churches, a Turkish mosque, several baths, and a palace, said to have been the residence of the last Armenian monarchs. All these display much splendour and architectural beauty, and the fretwork of some of the arches is very rich; but it is evident that the public buildings alone were on this massive scale, and that the private dwellings were always very humble. The hollows in the ground, and the mounds of loose stones scattered over the whole area of the city would lead me to suppose that they were much of the same style as those now in use. Throughout the whole of Armenia and Georgia I have remarked that, while the villages are scarcely raised above the level of the ground, the churches are massive structures visible from a great distance.[2]

Wilbraham does not always travel with such elevated and antiquarian aims in sight. He likes the people and their ways; at one point he exclaims: 'The Armenians are a wonderful nation, and it is much to be regretted that their early history should be involved in so much obscurity.'[3] (This was an unusual sentiment from a British officer of the time; most of them looked down on the Christian Armenians as non-combatants within the Islamic empires). Travelling in the heart of Turkish Armenia, Wilbraham writes:

> The plain of Moush is thickly studded with villages. They are almost all Armenian, but in the winter the nomad Kurds of the district (who, during the summer, pasture their flocks in the distant mountains) are quartered upon the villagers. Large quantities of tobacco are cultivated on the banks of the Kara Su, and some portion of it finds its way even to the bazaars of Constantinople.
>
> At three hours from Moush I halted for a few moments to change my baggage cattle. I had alighted, and was standing apart from the crowd, when an old man approached me, and, giving me a significant look, pinched my arm. This I found to be a sort of masonic sign among Armenians, to intimate that wine is to be had. Xenophon, in the description of his march through Armenia, speaks of 'old wines exceeding fragrant', which he met with in some of the villages; but either he was in greater luck than I was, or his palate was less fastidious. The sun had just set as I entered Arkavank, a straggling village on the bank of the Kara Su.
>
> It was curious, while traversing the same country which Xenophon passed through more than two thousand years before, to read his description of the mode of living of the inhabitants, and to remark how much of that description is applicable even at the present day, after the lapse of so many centuries. Their houses were then as now under ground, and were tenanted by their flocks and herds, as well as by their families. The Armenians of the present day seem indeed to differ little in their manner of life from their ancestors, excepting that they have lost some of the luxuries which their forefathers enjoyed. Besides the 'old wine' to which I have already alluded, Xenophon speaks of a species of 'malt liquor', preserved in earthen jars, a beverage of which I could find no traces in modern Armenia.[4]

CONSUL JAMES BRANT, *JOURNAL OF THE ROYAL GEOGRAPHICAL SOCIETY*, VOL. 10, 1841

The *JRGS* of 1841 contains four important accounts of lengthy travels through Turkish Armenia. They discuss inter-ethnic relations, the effects of war, government attitudes, especially in the field of taxation, and contain copious geographical details. The most important of the four is that of James Brant, British consul in Erzerum. In the summer of 1838 he had travelled south from Erzerum to Moush, then west to Kharput; returning to Moush by a different route, he travelled east to Bitlis, then on to Van, continuing along the northern shore of Lake Van; passing the sources of the Eastern Euphrates, he reached Bayazid, under the shadow of Mount Ararat, before taking the direct track westwards back to Erzerum. His account, of a little under 100 pages, repays close study, especially in the still-disputed matter of population statistics. (In two 'pashaliks', that is, provinces, those of Moush and Van, he noted that the Armenians outnumbered the Muslims: this was so after an extensive migration of Armenians from the region to Russian Armenia following the Treaty of Adrianople of 1829. See pages 351 and 395 of the journal.)

Consul Brant's narrative is not easy to quote from; however he was present at the festival of the Holy Virgin at Merek, north-east of Van, near the shore of the lake, in August of 1838, and his account is interesting and vivid. This shows, in the first place, an element of joy and festivity in the life of Turkish Armenians. Their existence has often been pictured as a continual round of sorrow and pain and injustice, and certainly these elements were very common; but a mild corrective is given in this account. It shows that the Turkish Armenians could be almost as festive as those in Persia, as recorded by Fryer. In the second place it shows that here at least good relations prevailed between Kurds and Armenians, at a time before such relations were destroyed by the interference of the government. And in the third place it shows, despite Consul Brant's objectivity in most things, that he was as archly Protestant as many of his successors in his observation of Armenian church 'superstition'.

> After following the lake for 2 miles we again struck inland behind a range of mountains which advance into the lake, and in about an hour reached Merek. Here is a monastery and church dedicated to the Virgin, whose festival was now celebrated. We passed a good many peasants, men, women and children, wending their way thither to join the festivities. We were 6 miles on the march from Ala-koy and, the road being good, I estimated the distance at about 20 miles. Merek is situated on the side of the mountains at a considerable elevation above the lake. Outside the village, I was met by some horsemen sent as a compliment by the Su-Bashi [police superintendent], who presides at the festival, to maintain order, and several bands of the rude music of the country also came out to meet me, not to do me honour but to obtain a present.
>
> The festival attracts people from all the surrounding country: the love of pleasure, however, has quite as much to do with their assembling as devotion. Dancing seemed to be the principal amusement of the women, of whom various groups were seen treading with solemn pace the circular

dance, to the usual sound of their harsh-sounding drum and fife. The women were all dressed in red cotton petticoats, with white cotton veils over their head reaching to the waist. The male portion of the assemblage were amused by the exhibition of dancing boys, or the antics of a bear. Every now and then came in a fresh party from a village, the chiefs of which were mounted on horses; the females followed on mules, asses or oxen, with their young children clinging around them. Music and young men dancing preceded the cavalcade. By similar parties the crowd kept hourly increasing: each set as it arrived took up the station allotted for its encampment on the side of a hill. The people were all in their holiday clothing: the display of finery, however, was very moderate, and the effect of it was not much improved by the dust collected on the journey. The scene was noisy enough, and certainly extraordinary, but the separation of the sexes renders such exhibitions very tame in eastern countries. In the evening the people thronged the small church even to suffocation, and while the service was going on fanatics were crying to the Virgin for relief from ills which no aid within their reach could alleviate, and endless crossings and prostrations attested, if not the piety of the devotees, at least their superstitious belief in the efficacy of their invocations ...

A little before sunset the Su-bashi mounted, and, attended by a concourse of Kurd horsemen, made the circuit of the tents. In a field below our camp, the Kurds for a short time amused themselves in their martial exercises, galloping and wheeling their coursers about, firing their pistols, brandishing their lances, advancing and retreating in mimic warfare, after which the whole cavalcade continued its progress. The dancing and music was kept up until after midnight, when the noisy crowd, exhausted by fatigue, sunk into repose.[5]

◯◯ CHAPTER 6 ◯◯

# 'A Healthy and a Hardy Race'
## James Morier and the Persian Armenians

James Morier (c. 1780–1849) was born in Smyrna of a Huguenot family. His father was a Levantine businessman. In 1807 he travelled from Turkey to Persia, to become personal assistant to the British ambassador. He grew to be steeped in the ways of the east, to which his wit and intelligence would not allow him to condescend. In 1815 he left Tehran and the diplomatic service, in order to devote himself fully to writing

Morier produced two volumes of travel, in 1812 and 1818. His fine and interesting *Second Journey* records events mostly of 1814, in which he had travelled in the company of the British ambassador, Sir Gore Ouseley. Ouseley had just assisted in negotiations for the treaty of Gulistan (1813), which had temporarily suspended hostilities between Russia and Persia. The party arrived in Yerevan in June – climatically speaking, a bad time. On the 15th they reached Echmiadzin, the centre of Armenian Christianity.

Here they were warmly welcomed by the Catholicos, Yeprem I, and the monks. The stateliness and style of the ambassadorial reception gave pleasure to the travellers. Morier's description is of a religious community unharassed by officialdom, and he especially noted the 'frankness and benignity' of the catholicos's expression.

The British party went to a 'short service' at the cathedral, where the monks sang in a full-voiced eastern manner, unusual to western ears, and the bells rang out raucously. At the conclusion of the service, the catholicos waved a golden crucifix at the British party in blessing.[1]

The heat was intense, and the party sought refuge in the mountains. Soon they reached Ashtarak, some 18 miles north of Echmiadzin. Here Morier was impressed by the local Armenian churches and monasteries, some of which were entire, others in ruins. He found much to admire both in their materials and in their workmanship.[2]

Persian Armenians feature elsewhere in Morier's narrative. He witnessed the run-down condition of the Armenians of New Julfa, but was hospitably received by an Armenian Catholic priest, living there in considerable poverty with his cat. He passed through villages in the vale of Khoi (north-west of Lake Urmia) which were mostly 'peopled by Armenians'[3]. The sight of Ararat moved him greatly: 'It is perfect in all its parts, no hard rugged feature, no unnatural prominences, every thing is in harmony, and all combines to render it one of the sublimest objects in nature.'[4] By the shores of Lake Sevan he sampled the famous trout,[5] and made drawings both of the Roman temple of Garni and the monastery of the Sacred Spear, Ayrivank, also known as Geghard.[6]

It is interesting to see how much of Morier's 1814 journey he incorporated into his fictional masterpiece, *Hajji Baba of Ispahan* (1824). In the novel we find descriptions of Armenian villages, customs and livelihood. The good humour of the catholicos and monks of Echmiadzin also features, as does the disruption caused by the Russo–Persian wars. Hajji Baba has been described by Sarah Searight as 'the great masterpiece of literature about the Middle East'. Lord Curzon described its eponymous hero as 'a Persian of the Persians; typical not merely of the life and surroundings, but of the character and instincts and manner of thought of his countrymen.' A Persian translation of the work was so successful and full of insight that, according to one authority (E. G. Browne), it was a cause – admittedly minor – of the Persian constitutional revolution of 1905.[7]

Hajji Baba, the unblushing and adventurous rogue who is the central character, starts life as the son of an Isfahan barber, and rises to become one of the shah's chief diplomats. The tone of the whole work is realistic, ironical and lively. It is far from being an oriental romance. In this extract the Hajji, currently sub-lieutenant to the shah's chief executioner, has paused with some companions at Ashtarak – just as Morier had found refuge there from the summer heat of Echmiadzin. Here the fictional group observe an immobile white figure and her male companion hiding within a ruined Armenian church. Hajji Baba requests the youth to tell his story.

> I am an Armenian by birth, and a Christian; my name is Yusuf. My father is chief of the village of Gavmishlu [the modern Jrashen], inhabited entirely by Armenians, situated not far from the beautiful river of Pembaki, and about six agatch [about 25 miles] from this place. In the middle of a verdant country, full of the richest pasturage, and enjoying a climate celebrated for its coolness and serenity, we are a healthy and a hardy race; and notwithstanding the numerous exactions of our governors, were happy in our poverty. We live so far within the mountains, that we are more distant from the tyranny usually exercised upon those who abide nearer great towns, the residences of governors; and, secluded from the world,

our habits are simple, and our modes of life patriarchal. I had an uncle, my father's brother, a deacon, and an attendant upon the head of our church, the patriarch at Etchmiazin; and another uncle, by my mother's side, was the priest of our village: therefore my family, being well in the church, determined that I should follow the sacred profession. My father himself, who subsisted by tilling the ground, and by his own labour had cleared away a considerable tract near the village, having two sons besides me, expected to receive sufficient help from them in the field, and therefore agreed to spare me for the church. Accordingly, when about ten years old, I went to Etchmiazin to be educated, where I learned to read, write, and perform the church service. I derived great pleasure from instruction, and read every book that came in my way. A very extensive library of Armenian books exists at the convent, of which I managed now and then to get a few; and although mostly on religious subjects, yet it happened that I once got a history of Armenia, which riveted all my attention; for I learnt by it that we were once a great nation, having kings, who made themselves respected in the world.

Reflecting upon our degraded state at the present day, and considering who were our governors, I became full of energy to shake off the yoke, and these feelings turned my thoughts from the sacred profession to which I was destined. About this time war broke out between Persia and Russia, and our village lying in the track of the armies marching to the frontiers, I felt that my family would require every protection possible, and that I should be more usefully employed with them than in a cloister. Accordingly, but a short time before taking priest's orders, I left my friends at Etchmiazin, and returned to my father's house. I was welcomed by everyone. Already had they felt the horrors of war; for marauding parties of both Persians and Russians (both equally to be feared) had made their appearance, and molested the peaceable and inoffensive inhabitants of ours and the neighbouring villages.

This frontier warfare, in its general results, was of no great utility to either of the powers; yet to those who inhabited the seat of it its consequences were dreadful. We were continually harassed either by the fears of the invading enemy, or by the exactions and molestations of the troops of our own government. Our harvests were destroyed, our cattle dispersed, and ourselves in instant danger of being carried away prisoners. Anxious to preserve our property, and our only resource to keep us from starvation, we continued to till our fields, but went to work with swords by our sides, and guns ready loaded on our backs; and when a stranger appeared, whoever he might be, we immediately assembled and made a show of defence. By this means, for several years, we managed, with great difficulty and perseverance, to get in our harvest, and, by the blessing of Providence, had enough to subsist upon. But here I must begin some of those particulars which relate to my individual history.

About two years ago, when securing our harvest, I had gone out long before dawn to reap the corn of one of our more distant fields, armed and prepared as usual. I perceived a Persian horseman, bearing a female behind him, and making great speed through a glen that wound nearly at the foot of a more elevated spot, upon which I was standing. The female evidently had been placed there against her will, for as soon as she perceived me she uttered loud shrieks, and extended her arms. I immediately flew down the craggy side of the mountain, and reached the lowermost part of the glen time enough to intercept the horseman's road. I called out to him to stop, and seconded my words by drawing my sword and putting myself in an attitude to seize his bridle as he passed. Embarrassed by the burden behind him, he was unable either to use his sword or the gun slung at his back, so he excited his horse to an increased speed, hoping thus to ride over me; but I stood my ground, and as I made a cut with my sabre, the horse bounded from the road with so sudden a start, that the frightened woman lost her hold and fell off. The horseman, free of his encumbrance, would now have used his gun; but, seeing mine already aimed at him, he thought it most prudent to continue his road, and I saw nothing more of him.

I ran to the assistance of the fallen woman, whom by her dress I discovered to be an Armenian. She was stunned and severely bruised: her outward veil had already disengaged itself, and, in order to give her air, I immediately pulled away the under veil which hides the lower part of the face (common to the Armenians) and, to my extreme surprise, beheld the most beautiful features that imagination can conceive. The lovely creature whom I supported in my arms was about fifteen years of age. Oh! I shall never forget the thrill of love, delight, and apprehension, which I felt at gazing upon her. I hung over her with all the intenseness of a first passion; a feeling arose in my heart which was new to me, and, forgetting everything but the object immediately before, I verily believe that I should have been for ever rooted to the spot, had she not opened her eyes, and begun to show signs of life. The first words she spoke went to my very soul; but when she discovered where she was and in the hands of an utter stranger, she began to cry and bewail herself in a manner that quite alarmed me. Little by little, however, she became more composed; and when she found that I was one of her own nation and religion, that I was moreover her deliverer, she began to look upon me with different feelings: my vanity made me hope that, perhaps, she was not displeased at the interest she had awakened in me.

One thing, however, she did not cease to deplore, and to upbraid me with: I had withdrawn her veil. There was no forgiveness for me: that indulgence which even a husband scarcely ever enjoys, that distinguishing emblem of chastity and honour so sacred in the eyes of an Armenian woman – every sense of decency had been disregarded by me, and I stood before her in the criminal character of one who had seen all her face. In vain I represented that had I not relieved her mouth and nose from the pressure of the lower band, she must have been suffocated; that her fall having deprived her of all sensation, had she not inhaled the fresh air death would have been the consequence. Nothing would convince her that she was not a lost woman. However, the following argument had more effect on her than any other: no one but myself was witness to her dishonour (if such she must call it); and I swore fervently by the Holy Cross, and by St Gregorio, that it should remain a profound secret in my heart as long as I had one to keep it in, that she permitted herself at length to be comforted.

The fair maiden, whose name we learn is Mariam, tells Yusuf her story: that she had been captured a few days earlier by a Persian horseman, following a skirmish between Persians and Georgians, and he had ridden wildly through the countryside with her. Eventually she grew brave enough to cry out; Yusuf had heard these cries and had rescued her. As she finishes the tale of her woe and her liberty, her brothers and uncle appear, and all congratulate her deliverer. Rapidly the tale spreads from village to village.

> At length it came out that she had been carried away by a giant, who had an iron head, claws and feet of steel, and scales on his back, mounted upon a beast that tore up the ground at every bound, and made noises in its rapid course like the discharges of artillery. They added to this, that of a sudden an angel, in the shape of a ploughboy, descended from the top of a high mountain in a cloud, and as he wielded a sword of fire in his hand, it frightened the horse, threw Mariam to the ground, and reduced the giant and his steed to ashes: for when she recovered from her fright they were no longer to be seen. I was pointed out as the illustrious ploughboy, and immediately the attention of the whole village was turned towards me; but, unfortunately, when about receiving nearly divine honours, a youth, whom I had frequently met while tending cattle in the mountains, recognized me, and said, 'He is no angel – he is Yusuf, the son of Coja Petros of Gavmishlu:' and thus I was reduced to my mortality once more.

Plans are made for the wedding of Yusuf and Mariam; but they are uneasily interrupted by warlike preparations throughout the region between Russians and Persians. Despite the threatening atmosphere, the wedding goes ahead. It is splendidly described by Morier, and the glittering account again demonstrates the centrality of the wedding ceremony in Armenian life. However, as the bride and bridegroom retire for their wedding night, they are most intolerably interrupted by a skirmish between Persians and Russians, part of which takes place in their actual wedding chamber. Morier's picture is an apt image of the life, peacefulness, pleasure and productivity of Armenians being destroyed by the brutality and violence of the surrounding empires, and of the destructive intrusiveness of those imperial entities, which, in the years before the rational system of nation-states, preyed upon the smaller nationalities for the sake of dynastic grandiosity, greed and macho image.

Yusuf's beloved bride is snatched away. Later, following brave and enterprising exploits, he discovers that she is held in the harem of the serdar, or Persian governor, of Yerevan. Yusuf posts himself besides the river Zengi, today known as the Hrazdan, searchingly looking up the precipice toward the dark rock upon which the harem is situated. The perpetual movement of troops gives him adequate cover for his observation; a Russian advance upon Yerevan is imminent. Every day he parades upon the bridge, which is in full view of the lattice-work of the harem window. Suddenly, the lattice opens, and a female looks out. It is she. In response he plunges unhesitatingly into the river below, where he is directly beneath her window. She withdraws, reappears, then leans out and jumps down, down into the river and to her husband. Her fall is broken by a willow tree sprouting from the rock face. He grabs her, takes her to safety, and flees as fast as he can to Ashtarak, until the two find rest in the ruined church where Hajji Baba met them.

Hajji Baba debates what to do. Yusuf had committed a crime punishable by death. He ought to be sent back to Yerevan. But the Hajji thinks better, and tells Yusuf that he will be excused this due process if he reconnoitres Russian positions in the area. To this the Armenian concurs. He explores the region of Hamamlu (the modern Spitak) with efficiency and accuracy.

Hajji Baba and his entourage make their way towards Utch Kilisse - Echmiadzin, seat of the Armenian Catholicos. He is, we are told, known by the title of khalifeh or caliph, 'a designation which, comprising the head of the civil as well as the religious government, the Mussulmans used formerly to bestow on the sovereigns who held their sway at Bagdad and elsewhere'. In amongst the monastic buildings of Echmiadzin the forces of the serdar are encamped, treating the Armenian clergy with rude indifference. Hajji Baba is cross-questioned by the serdar about Russian troop movements, and is compelled to come clean with the whole story of Yusuf, Mariam, and the young Armenian's fearless and accurate reconnoitring of Russian positions.

The serdar, smiling through a malevolent appearance, admits that 'the Armenian had performed wonders'. He demands that Yusuf be brought in, and the catholicos too. Both are ordered to give account for this behaviour. This is Yusuf's answer:

> If I am guilty of having taken aught from any man, save my own, here am I, ready to answer for myself with my life. She who threw herself out of

your windows into my arms was my wife before she was your slave. We are both the Shah's rayats, and it is best known to yourself if you can enslave them or no. We are Armenians, 'tis true, but we have the feelings of men. It is well known to all Persia that our illustrious Shah has never forced the harem of even the meanest of his subjects; and, secure in that feeling, how could I ever suppose, most noble serdar, that we should not receive the same protection under your government? You were certainly deceived when told that she was a Georgian prisoner; and had you known that she was the wife of one of your peasantry, you would never have made her your property.

The catholicos grows alarmed at Yusuf's language; but the wily and villainous-looking serdar looks pleased, restores his wife to him, and tells Yusuf that he is to be his servant. 'All congratulated the serdar on his humanity and his benevolence.'

Yusuf is less than happy in his role as servant of the serdar. He is compelled to wear long and extravagant garments of crimson velvet trimmed with gold braid – very different from the short tunic of old. He feels feminized. He hates being the idle appendage of the governor, and tells the Hajji not to be offended if he sooner or later declines the honour of serving him. 'Better live a swineherd in the Georgian mountains, naked and houseless, than in all these silks and velvets, a despised hanger-on.'

Hajji Baba's superior, the chief executioner, and the serdar are emboldened to risk an encounter with Russian forces (two artillerymen, firing alternately) in which they acquit themselves with no distinction. Over-eager to push forward their cavalry, they entirely neglect infantry. The result is a rout. Suddenly the governor wonders: where is his servant Yusuf? But Yusuf and Mariam, together with all their large extended family and their moveable property, have by then migrated *en masse* into Russian territory. When, later, the serdar's forces seek out their village, intent on pillage and destruction, they find only tilled fields. Everything else has been moved to Russia. The Armenian emigrants were well received by their new hosts, who allotted them lands and gave them every help in re-establishing their livelihood.[8]

## CHAPTER 7

### 'Would That You Would Love Me'
### An Armenian Lesson on the Heath

A few decades later Armenia became, in a somewhat oblique and off-beat manner, entwined in the plots of two more works of English fiction. The context was linguistic, speculative, alternative and largely non-political, although there was a summons to liberty. In 1851 George Borrow (1803–81) wrote a semi-autobiographical novel entitled *Lavengro*. Its sequel, *The Romany Rye*, appeared six years later. The *Oxford Companion to English Literature* describes Borrow's novels as having 'a peculiar picaresque quality, graphically presenting a succession of gypsies, rogues, strange characters, and adventurers of all kinds, without much coherence, the whole permeated with the spirit of the "wind on the heath" and of the unconventional.'

This sums up the world of *Lavengro* and *The Romany Rye*. The novels are in a way the mid nineteenth-century equivalents of *Withnail and I*. At the time they derived some of their fame from being rough-hewn creations written in an age of gentility and refinement. Borrow was fascinated by road people, individuals dedicated to proto-hippy, open-air lifestyles, governed by happenstance and without too much dedication to work. He sought out and articulated the cussed individuality of the English, defining it and showing its strange splendour, before it became smothered in the world of hunt balls and smart marriages. The world represented in his novels is largely that of England before industrialization, a time congenial for roguish characters. He was especially fond of the Gypsies, their language, and theories on the outer edges of linguistic derivation. (The word 'Lavengro' is Romany for 'philologist')

The Armenian people caught Borrow's attention on account of their language, and from certain individual, out-of-the-way qualities that he perceived they manifested. Borrow knew some basic, if slightly inaccurate, Armenian, which he had learnt in his teens in Norwich Public Library. In *The Romany Rye* there is a reference to 'old Villotte, from whose work I first contrived to pick up the rudiments of Armenian'. Père Jacques Villotte was a French Jesuit, who had travelled widely, and compiled a 700-page Armenian–Latin dictionary which was published in Rome in 1713.

In the earlier of the novels, Lavengro, the eponymous narrator, discourses in a florid and speculative manner on the connections between the words for 'bread' in various languages. He then expounds on the Armenian term for it to a new acquaintance, a merchant who turns out, by a miracle of coincidence, to be an Armenian himself. 'By the Patriarch and the Three Holy Churches, this is wonderful! How came you to know aught of my language?', exclaims the merchant, whose stolen pocket-book the narrator had recovered.

The two discuss the Armenian words for bread and wine (z-hats and kini; z- is the accusative prefix in ancient Armenian), and decide to partake of the same. The Armenian merchant explains that he is the son of a native of Isfahan, Persia: that is, one of the Armenian merchant community founded in New Julfa by Shah Abbas in 1605, and which John Fryer vividly described in 1677. The Armenian and the Englishman discuss some English words derived, via a philological genealogy which would not be acceptable today, from Armenian. Admiration is heaped on the Armenian language – 'noble and energetic', 'bold and expressive'. The narrator is asked by the Armenian merchant to translate some Armenian fables, a commission which he declines, whereupon he takes leave of his new acquaintance.[1]

The Armenian returns in the novel, after digressions on Danish ballads, Welsh verse and French dancing. He is not given a name. He narrates the more recent history of the country: how, after the fall of the monarchy, power both spiritual and temporal had devolved on the leaders of the Armenian Church, a power which had been much circumscribed by the Islamic empires. He relates too how the pope had sent emissaries to Ararat, 'seducing the minds of weak-willed people' (Borrow always enjoyed a jibe at Roman Catholicism), 'persuading them that the hillocks of Rome are higher than the ridges of Ararat ... and that puny Latin is a better language than nervous and sonorous Haik [Armenian]'. The Armenian's parting shot at a particularly importunate emissary of Rome some time earlier had been a fervent assertion that 'the roots of Ararat are deeper than those of Rome'[2] – a sentiment which is repeated later in the novel.[3]

Lavengro lives on the edge of penury. He thinks that he might after all translate Armenian fables – anything to make a few shillings. One day however he chides his Armenian acquaintance for amassing a fortune in London, and doing nothing to liberate his countrymen from their imperial bondage. What does his patriotism mean, if the people live in slavery? The merchant replies 'Hem!' The next day, as Lavengro returns to his Armenian friend, to accept the commission of the translation, he finds a note addressed to him, saying that he has indeed taken the words to heart, and has departed to take up the sword and fight his people's oppressor.[4] So the narrator is left, without his commission for translation, to survive on his wits with an almost empty pocket.

Nothing happens; little is accomplished; and the Armenian never returns. Lavengro teaches a little Armenian to his beautiful Isopel (or Belle), who had helped him to victory in a brawl with the Flaming Tinman. The two find themselves discussing the possibility of declining the Armenian nouns for 'master' and 'mistress' in the open air. A storm growls in the background, the heathland is rent by a flash of lightning, and a carriage overturns. In this way, without an ending, the novel ends.

In the companion work, *The Romany Rye*, Lavengro resolves to teach more Armenian grammar to his beloved Belle. Perhaps the question for the reader is: who is giving instruction to whom?

'Have you been far?' said Belle. 'Merely to that public-house,' said I, 'to which you directed me on the second day of our acquaintance.' 'Young men should not make a habit of visiting public-houses,' said Belle, 'they are bad places. 'They may be so to some people,' said I, 'but I do not think the worst public-house in England could do me any harm.' 'Perhaps you are so bad already,' said Belle, with a smile, 'that it would be impossible to spoil you.' 'How dare you catch at my words?' said I; 'come, I will make you pay for doing so – you shall have this evening the longest lesson in Armenian that I have ever inflicted on you.' 'You may well say inflicted,' said Belle, 'but pray spare me. I do not wish to hear anything about Armenian, especially this evening.' 'Why this evening?' said I. Belle made no answer. 'I will not spare you,' said I; 'this evening I intend to make you conjugate an Armenian verb.' 'Well, be it so,' said Belle; 'for this evening you shall command.' 'To command is *hramahyel*,' said I. 'Ram her ill, indeed,' said Belle; 'I do not wish to begin with that.' 'No,' said I, 'as we have come to the verbs, we will begin regularly; *hramahyel* is a verb of the second conjugation. We will begin with the first.' 'First of all tell me,' said Belle, 'what a verb is?' 'A part of speech,' said I, 'which, according to the dictionary, signifies some action or passion; for example, I command you, or I hate you.' 'I have given you no cause to hate me,' said Belle, looking me sorrowfully in the face.

'I was merely giving two examples,' said I, 'and neither was directed at you. In those examples, to command and hate are verbs. Belle, in Armenian there are four conjugations of verbs; the first ends in *al*, the second in *yel*, the third in *oul* and the fourth in *il*. Now, have you understood me?'

'I am afraid it will all end ill,' said Belle. 'Hold your tongue,' said I, 'or you will make me lose my patience.' 'You have already made me nearly lose mine,' said Belle. 'Let us have no unprofitable interruptions,' said I;

'the conjugations of the Armenian verbs are neither so numerous nor so difficult as the declensions of the nouns; hear that, and rejoice. Come, we will begin with the verb *hntal,* a verb of the first conjugation, which signifies to rejoice. Come along; *hntam,* I rejoice; *hntas,* thou rejoicest; why don't you follow, Belle?'

'I am sure I don't rejoice, whatever you may do,' said Belle. 'The chief difficulty, Belle,' said I, 'that I find in teaching you the Armenian grammar, proceeds from your applying to yourself and me every example I give. Rejoice, in this instance, is merely an example of an Armenian verb of the first conjugation, and has no more to do with your rejoicing than *lal,* which is also a verb of the first conjugation, and which signifies to weep, would have to do with your weeping, provided I made you conjugate it. Come along; *hntam,* I rejoice; *hntas,* thou rejoicest; *hnta,* he rejoices; *hntamk,* we rejoice: now, repeat those words.'

'I can't,' said Belle, 'they sound more like the language of horses than human beings. Do you take me for – ?' 'For what?' said I. Belle was silent. 'Were you going to say mare?' said I. 'Mare! mare! by the bye, do you know that mare in old English stands for woman; and that when we call a female an evil mare, the strict meaning of the term is merely a bad woman. So if I were to call you a mare without prefixing bad, you must not be offended.' 'But I should though,' said Belle. 'I was merely attempting to make you acquainted with a philological fact,' said I. 'If mare, which in old English, and likewise in vulgar English, signifies a woman, sounds the same as mare, which in modern and polite English signifies a female horse, I can't help it. There is no confusion of sounds in Armenian, not, at least, in the same instance. Belle, in Armenian, woman is *ghin,* the same word, by the by, as our queen, whereas mare is *madagh tzi,* which signifies a female horse; and perhaps you will permit me to add, that a hard-mouthed jade is, in Armenian, *madagh tzi hsdierah.*'

'I can't bear this much longer,' said Belle. 'Keep yourself quiet,' said I; 'I wish to be gentle with you; and to convince you, we will skip *hntal,* and also for the present verbs of the first conjugation and proceed to the second. Belle, I will now select for you to conjugate the prettiest verb in Armenian; not only of the second, but also of all the four conjugations; that verb is *siriel.* Here is the present tense: – *siriem, siries, sire, siriemk, sirek, sirien.* You observe that it runs on just in the same manner as *hntal,* save and except that the *e* is substituted for *a;* and it will be as well to tell you that almost the only difference between the second, third and fourth conjugation, and the first, is the substituting in the present, preterite and other tenses *e* or *ou,* or *i* for *a;* so you see that the Armenian verbs are by no means difficult. Come on, Belle, and say *siriem.*' Belle hesitated. 'Pray oblige me, Belle, by saying *siriem!*' Belle still appeared to hesitate. 'You must admit, Belle, that it is much softer than *hntam.*' 'It is so,' said Belle; 'and to oblige you I will say *siriem.*'

'Very well indeed, Belle,' said I. 'No *vartabied*, or doctor, could have pronounced it better; and now, to show you how verbs act upon pronouns in Armenian, I will say *siriem zkiez*. Please to repeat *siriem zkiez!*' '*Siriem zkiez!*' said Belle; 'that last word is very hard to say.' 'Sorry that you think so, Belle,' said I. 'Now please to say *siria zis*.' Belle did so. 'Exceedingly well,' said I. 'Now say, *Yerani the sireir zis*.' '*Yerani the sireir zis*,' said Belle; 'Capital!' said I; 'you have now said, I love you – love me – ah! would that you would love me!'

'And I have said all these things?' said Belle. 'Yes,' said I; 'you have said them in Armenian.' 'I would have said them in no language that I understood,' said Belle; 'and it was very wrong of you to take advantage of my ignorance, and make me say such things.' 'Why so?' said I; 'if you said them, I said them too.' 'You did so,' said Belle; 'but I believe you were merely bantering and jeering.' 'As I told you before, Belle,' said I, 'the chief difficulty which I find in teaching you Armenian proceeds from your persisting in applying to yourself and me every example I give.' 'Then you meant nothing after all,' said Belle, raising her voice.

'Let us proceed,' said I; '*sirietsi*, I loved.' 'You never loved anyone but yourself,' said Belle; 'and what's more – ' '*Sirietsits*, I will love,' said I; '*sirietsies*, thou wilt love.' 'Never one so thoroughly heartless,' said Belle. 'I tell you what, Belle, you are becoming intolerable, but we will change the verb; or rather I will now proceed to tell you here, that some of the Armenian conjugations have their anomalies; one species of these I wish to bring before your notice. As old Villotte says – from whose work I first contrived to pick up the rudiments of Armenian – "*Est verborum transitivorum, quorum infinitivus* – " but I forgot, you don't understand Latin. He says there are certain transitive verbs, whose infinitive is in *outsaniel*; the preterite in *outsi*; the imperative in *oue*; for example – *parghatsoutsaniem*, I irritate –'

'You do, you do,' said Belle; 'and it will be better for both of us, if you leave off doing so.'

'You would hardly believe, Belle,' said I, 'that the Armenian is in some respects closely connected with the Irish, but so it is; for example that word *parghatsoutsaniem* is evidently derived from the same root as *feargaim*, which, in Irish, is as much as to say I vex.'

'You do, indeed,' said Belle, sobbing.

'But how do you account for it?'

'O man, man!' said Belle, bursting into tears, 'for what purpose do you ask a poor ignorant girl such a question, unless it be to vex and irritate her? If you wish to display your learning, do so to the wise and instructed and not to me, who can scarcely read or write …'

Belle knows that they have reached an impasse, although Lavengro believes their life will continue as before, despite having given her a lesson in which he had been keener to boss than to teach. His heedless display of linguistic skill had been too narcissistic to allow for an understanding of Belle, the feminine other. 'Our ways lie different,' she says to him simply. He still believes that their love affair can be saved, and begs her to join him in a new life in America. He offers to prove his love by wrestling with her, as Sygurd, the serpent killer, had wrestled with Brynhilda – an attempt, made too late, to find something definably equal in his feelings, and to show actual awareness of her female otherness. But she is not convinced, and the next day she leaves, never to return.[5]

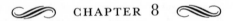

CHAPTER 8

# 'The Groaning and Complaining
## of Neighbouring Quadrupeds'
### Armenian Village Life in the Ottoman Empire

Before the destruction of the Ottoman Armenian community, initiated in the 1890s and completed during the first world war, Armenians were overwhelmingly a peasant agricultural people. It has been estimated that 70 per cent of the population lived on the land. This people, living in its land continuously since before the time of Xenophon's *Anabasis*, constituted the backbone of the Armenian nation. Such people still live on in the towns and villages of Armenia and Mountainous Karabagh today.

Little heed was paid to the peasant Armenians, except by perceptive writers and travellers such as Morier. Most observers, including some class-conscious British, disliked Armenians, seeing them as 'mere' trades-men who saw no military service. Within the Ottoman empire, there was in fact no possibility of a military career, since they were Christians. Until 1908 no Ottoman non-Muslim people was permitted to bear arms, so the lack of a martial tradition among the Ottoman Armenians was not something for which they were responsible. It is noteworthy that, when individual Armenians entered a more equitable society, such as imperial Russia, and were able to take up a military career, they showed themselves to be excellent soldiers – as is seen by the example of the four Armenian generals on the Caucasian front during the war of 1877–78 – Loris-Melikov, Ter-Gukasov, Lazarev and Shelkovnikov.

Prejudiced travellers ignored the existence of the Armenian peasantry. They wanted to see, and so they saw, Armenians only as money-making middlemen – as townspeople doing deals. Today such high-born visitors would be seen as snobbish, boorish, intellectual louts; but in Victorian times they were listened to, as they discoursed volubly on the difference between 'martial races', and 'trading races'. In order to give a semblance of justification to such myths, the peasant with his husbandry and flocks was ignored.

The peasantry was also on occasion kept out of focus by the urban and

56

metropolitan Armenians, who, in moments of forgetful embarrassment, sometimes chose to pass over the existence of the rural communities with their animals.

During the Russo–Turkish war of 1877–78 there were a number of British correspondents in Ottoman lands. The war was covered in as much detail as the Crimean War, and much of the material gathered by the journalists was if anything of greater interest; but whereas William Russell's dispatches from the Crimea have frequently been reprinted, *The War Correspondence of the Daily News* of 1877–78 has not. Seven correspondents covered the war for the *News*, and a number of the dispatches appear from Turkey-in-Asia, parts of which constituted Turkish Armenia.

One of the correspondents (they are indicated by symbols, but there is no key in the published work for decoding the symbols into human identities) sent home dispatches from Erzerum during the winter of 1877–78, while waiting for the Russians to attack. In a dispatch dated from Illidge (Ilidja, or Ilica, west of Erzerum), on 4 December 1877, the correspondent wrote:

> Winter has set darkly in over Armenia; and every day we marvel more and more how the Russians can hold their own against the weather away up the Deve Boyun mountains, notwithstanding even their felt-covered tents and well-supplied stoves. We who are down in the plain, that is merely 6,000 feet above the sea level, cannot help speculating on the feelings of the beleaguering force, perched on ridges a couple of thousand feet above us ...
>
> While awaiting the grave circumstances which any moment may produce, perhaps a description of an Armenian village, far away from the limits of European civilization, may be acceptable. I rode from Erzerum to Illidge in two hours. I crossed a wide bleak plain, blinding white with newly fallen snow. At Guez [modern Gez], an intermediate village, I drew up to have a cup of coffee. My semi-military garb created a certain amount of suspicion. 'Who knows,' thought the villagers, 'but that this is only an excuse to enter an *oda* [room], and once there, he is quartered on us.' Such, it seems, is their experience of Ottoman officers. However, my horses standing unbridled and unpacked at the door somewhat re-assured them, and for a backsheesh I got a couple of cups of unsugared coffee. A few words of question and answer. 'Have the Russian patrols been here?' 'No, pasha,' was the reply. This I knew to be untrue, but in my hypothetic character these poor Armenians were not supposed to speak the absolute truth. From certain information, I knew that the Cossacks had been there but two evenings previously to requisition hay and oats. I went on.
>
> An expanse of marshy land, and a bridge which at a distance looked like that of a railway. Then came this village, Illidge. It looks like a place

that once was populous, as the sense goes here. Now there are empty houses and deserted – thoroughfares, I suppose I must say. Streets they could never be called even in the best of times. Here and there a few suspicious-looking ducks and hens wandered, and occasionally an inhabitant peered cautiously round the angle of a snow-heaped dwelling. The newly arrived horsemen might be Cossacks, or, worse still the Karapapakhs of Muhir Ali [border guerillas, who also terrorized Ottoman Armenian villagers]. A short parley, and the bolder of the inhabitants who ventured forth were convinced that we were neither one nor the other. As a result we were shown to the house of the chief man of the place, an unhappy individual who, be the newcomers Christians or Mussulmans, is responsible for everything.

Then we entered the chief man's house. It was a low, long building, the walls seven feet high, of rough stone rudely piled. The flat earth roof was thickly covered with snow. A long passage led to a stable, occupied by half a dozen cows, buffalo calves, and horses. An odour of ammonia exhaled from the place. In one corner, and separated only by a low, wooden partition, was the *oda*, the 'guest chamber'. A kind of pathway ran up its midst conducting to a stove-like fire-place, where cattle droppings, kneaded with earth, smouldered dimly. On either side the pathway were bands of wood, indicating the divans, where a kind of rush matting covered the beaten earth up to the rough wall. A mattress, two pillows, and a stuffed cotton quilt were luxuries accorded to the stranger guest.

The level of the floors being considerably below that of the ground outside, and the roof of rough beams arched slightly, the chamber had a much larger and airier appearance than could be expected within the squat semi-subterranean building one looked at from the outside. In a kind of low gable opposite the fireplace, a single window eight inches square, and closed with white greased paper, admitted a dim light. Coming in from the blinding glare of the snowy plain, it was like entering a coal-cellar. At one's elbow, shut off only by a partition 18 inches high, cows and calves munched their chopped straw. To inhabit the *oda* of an Armenian peasant's house is literally to inhabit a stable. All the sights, sounds, and odours of a rude, close stable are palpable to a degree far from pleasant. From the space outside the stable door ran long corridors of unplastered, uncemented rubble masonry, leading to the different chambers.

The *oda* of the female portion of the family was a great square chamber 30 feet either way, roofed with the peculiar kind of cupola common in these countries. Great beams cross diagonally above the corners; others cross these in an opposite sense, each tier advancing more than that below it over the centre of the room, till after six or seven tiers, a dome is formed having in its summit a square opening, through which come air and light. There are a great many other chambers, devoted to storing grain, chopped straw, and hay, and agricultural implements.

These houses are admirably adapted to the extremes of temperature of this climate. In summer the thick walls and earth-covered roofs keep the rooms comparatively cool; and when, as now, the cold is almost insupportable outside, the *oda*, under the joint influence of dung-fire and the animals collected alongside, is quite warm. Owing to this mild temperature within the chambers, even now the stray flies are to be seen; and, I am sorry to add, other more objectionable specimens of insect creation.

All night long one is disturbed by the groaning and complaining of the neighbouring quadrupeds; and long ere dawn shows faintly athwart the paper square in the gable, the plaintive lowing of hungry calves, and the angry cries of quarrelsome horses, break one's rest. Even now, at ten at night, various animals wander incontinently to and fro; and not five minutes ago I was obliged to repel by physical force an incursion on the part of a large black ass, who walked solemnly in with a view of partaking of a bag of oats, which constitutes my impromptu writing-table. A calf is munching the end of a rush mat on which I sit, and I am obliged to keep an eye on a large black rat, who has serious designs on a cold fowl in the corner. At meal-times I am subjected to a new species of mortification. The elders of the village, accompanied by a large following, sit or stand outside the low railing at the end of the *oda*, and gaze upon my proceedings with the absorbed interest of a rustic witnessing for the first time some soul-stirring drama. As these people speak but little Turkish, and that with Armenian idiom, our conversation is necessarily limited. The little Turkish I know is classical beside that of these people.[1]

There is a contrast between the oppressed, suspicious village life described here and the vital, energized, gun-at-the-ready village life described by Morier in his fact-based novel set across the international border; and there is an even greater distance from Armenian life west of Erzerum to that of the Armenians of New Julfa at the time of Shah Abbas, although a mild corrective appeared in James Brant's description of the Van festival. In Morier's account, Armenians were seen making decisions about their own fate, and challenging authority, but in the villages of Ottoman lands they appear most frequently as victims, weighed down by the seeming irrevocability of tyranny – a tyranny which might briefly lift, but for no more than the duration of a religious festival. Maybe there was some essential difference between the administration of Sunni Turk and Shii Persian. Maybe, in the context of Shah Abbas, the important distinction was between a ruler who valued the talents of one of his minorities, and a ruling tradition which found no place for admiration of anything outside the compass of the ruling faith and ethnicity. The distinction, too, between Ottoman control, and Persian tolerance of diversity, is something that also emerges from the comparison: that the

Ottomans sought at all times to be in command of the non-Turkish communities, whereas the Persians felt less need for total over-all control. Whatever the reason, it is hard to avoid the impression of gloom, oppression and unease from descriptions of Ottoman Armenian village life.

# CHAPTER 9

## 'A Consciousness of Some Heavy Responsibility' Gladstone, the Duke Of Argyll, Curzon and William Watson

There was a contradiction within British foreign policy towards the Ottoman empire in the nineteenth century. On the one hand, in 1828 the Duke of Wellington had unhesitatingly called the battle of Navarino, by which Greece had gained its freedom from the Ottoman realm, an 'untoward event'. To him the empire was 'our ancient ally' – an allusion to Queen Elizabeth's dealings with Sultan Murad III in the 1580s.

But at the same time Britain saw herself as an upholder of freedom, the opponent of tyranny and autocracy, the cradle of free opinions. However, if some liberality had been discerned within Ottoman Turkey in the mid nineteenth century, by the end it had been snuffed out, and the sultan's dominions had become tyrannical and spy-ridden. Britain then found it difficult to extricate itself from association with Turkey, and the sultan's treatment of his non-Turkish national communities proved an embarrassment to his principal foreign backer.

The situation was complicated by the fact that the British empire was, from about 1870, perceived as possessing a moral quality. Britain was a moral nation. For Gladstone this perception was given definition by a deeply held Anglican faith. Politics without an ethical system based on religion held no meaning for him. Others who expressed an opinion, such as the poet William Watson, held that the pursuit of international morality was the only justification for the British empire.

But opponents, such as Disraeli in the period 1875–78, and Queen Victoria throughout her life, gave support to the Ottoman empire as a matter of first principle, with little regard to how it treated its subjects. They saw it as a buffer state to imperial Russia, and crucial in securing British interests in India. Queen Victoria, whose moody comments on the situation alternated between loftiness and hysteria, once expressed the view that even criticism of Turkey might bring about the demise of the highest moral power, the British empire.

To Gladstone regional arguments were of less significance. His powerful and energetic Christian belief led him initially to support Ottoman Christians, as Christians struggling within a Muslim empire. His moral conscience later broadened, and his opposition to Ottoman power grew to be non-sectarian. He came to loathe the sultan's government not on account of its Islamic principles but because of its cruelty and deception. On the matter of Russia, he believed that the fears of his Tory opponents could be allayed by negotiation, not by confrontation (a view which ultimately prevailed with the creation of the Triple Entente), and certainly not by supporting a state which treated its subjects in the way that imperial Turkey did, merely because it bordered Russia. However, for various reasons of state Gladstone's urgings failed, and the Ottoman empire was left free to kill its Armenian subjects in 1894–96. At this time, Gladstone, in his mid 80s, became immersed in their fate.

It could also be reasonably argued that Britain held some measure of responsibility for the massacres of the 1890s. A sense of guilt was to some extent appropriate. The viewpoint of Gladstonian Liberals was not all high-flown Victorian moralizing. Gladstone had a clear understanding of the diplomatic and legal basis of the manner in which Ottoman Turkey had been accepted into the comity of nations, much of which he had expounded at length in speeches in the course of the Midlothian Campaign of 1879. Another leading Victorian Liberal statesman, the Duke of Argyll, also spelt out Britain's unique responsibility from the same legal-diplomatic perspective, basing his arguments on his understanding of the terms of the treaty of Paris and the Cyprus Convention.

Nevertheless, Gladstone always sought the agreement of the rest of Europe. He believed Europe had to act in a united manner, otherwise nothing would be done to improve the condition of the peoples of the Ottoman empire, especially the Christian peasantry, who suffered more than the rest, since they were unarmed and endured double taxation. (They were taxed by their feudal masters, and by the officials installed following the empire's re-organization.) Other members of the Concert of Europe were less committed to Armenian reforms – especially the Kaiser's Germany, which from 1883 refused to go along with Britain in pressing the Ottoman government to keep its word on making changes. Conditions in the Ottoman east deteriorated, and the Armenians responded by creating organizations which were initially committed to self-defence and later to revolution.

## W. E. GLADSTONE

It has to be said, too, that a portion of the blame for the appalling situation of the mid 1890s lay with Gladstone himself, since he had, in

1882, removed certain special British consuls who had been posted in the region by Disraeli's administration. Gladstone had seen their presence as an example of Britain stepping out of line, and of acting alone in a matter which should have been the united concern of all the great powers. He made his decision from the best of motives, seeking to instil a structure of law into international relations; but the net result of withdrawing the consuls had been to leave the minorities (especially the Armenians) more exposed to local oppression. Gladstone's concern with the theoretical model prevented him from offering help to the oppressed in a practical, day-to-day manner. He failed to see that law was inseparable from its enforcement.

In 1894 there was a minor uprising in Sasun, in Turkish Armenia, followed by a major massacre perpetrated by troops and their local irregulars. The events were sparked off by the persistence of feudal relations between the dominant Kurds and their retainer-Armenians, coupled with the introduction of the 'new' methods of central government, which meant heavy taxation violently enforced, and with, as a background, a continuing attitude on the part of the authorities and their local surrogates that the Armenians were merely infidels who should know their place. Despite the presence of government agents sent there to keep inquisitive journalists out, the truth about the repression became known, owing to the persistence of some journalists, chief of whom was the Irishman E. J. Dillon. Dillon was a brilliant linguist and scholar, fluent in about 12 languages (including Zend). Working for the *Daily Telegraph*, he was also a dedicated investigator, whom no governmental wile could block. He reached Armenia disguised as a Russian officer, and wrote a devastating account of conditions for the *Contemporary Review*.[1]

The Ottoman government was compelled to hold a commission on the events in the town of Moush. A frightful series of official pogroms of Armenians followed in late 1895 throughout the empire. Gladstone became deeply involved with the Armenian issue at this time. On 29 December 1894, his eighty-fifth birthday, he had received a deputation of Armenians at Hawarden, to whom he spoke with great eloquence. This meeting was followed by two great speeches, at Chester and Liverpool, the latter being made at the age of 86. The meeting at Chester was convened on 6 August 1895; the Duke of Westminster presided. Part of what Gladstone said is as follows:

> It is perfectly true that the government whose deeds we have to impeach is a Mahomedan government, and it is perfectly true that the sufferers under those outrages, under those inflictions, are Christian sufferers. The Mahomedan subjects of Turkey suffer a great deal, but what they suffer is

only in the way of the ordinary excesses and defects of an intolerably bad government – perhaps the worst on the face of the earth. That which we have now to do is, I am sorry to say, the opening up of an entirely new chapter. It is not a question of indifferent laws indifferently enforced. It is not a question of administrative violence and administrative abuse. It cuts further and goes to the root of all that concerns human life in its elementary conditions. But this I will say, that if, instead of dealing with the Turkish government and impeaching it for its misdeeds towards Christian subjects, we were dealing with a Christian government that was capable of similar misdeeds towards Mahomedan subjects, our indignation ought not to be less, but greater, than it is now ...

Now it was my fate, I think some six or more months ago, to address a very limited number of Armenian gentlemen and gentlemen interested in Armenia on this subject, and at that time I ventured to point out that one of our duties was to avoid premature judgements. There was no authoritative and impartial declaration before the world at that time on the subject of what is known as the Sasun massacre, that massacre to which the noble duke has alluded and with respect to which, horrible as that massacre was, one of the most important witnesses in this case declares that it is thrown into the shade and has become pale and ineffective by the side of the unspeakable horrors which are being enacted from month to month, from week to week, and day to day in the different provinces of Armenia.

It was a duty to avoid premature judgement, and I think it was avoided. There was a great reserve, but at last the engine of dispassionate enquiry was brought to bear, and then it was found that another duty, very important in general in these cases, really in this particular instance had no particular place at all, and though it is a duty to avoid exaggeration, a most sacred duty, it is a duty that has little or no place in the case before us, because it is too well known that the powers of language hardly suffice to describe what has been and is being done, and that exaggeration, if we were ever so much disposed to it, is in such a case really beyond our power.

Those are dreadful words to speak. It is a painful office to perform, and nothing but a strong sense of duty could gather us together between these walls or could induce a man of my age and a man who is not wholly without other difficulties to contend with to resign for a moment that repose and quietude which is the last of many great earthly blessings remaining to him in order to invite you to enter into a consideration of this question – I will not say in order to invite yourself to be flooded with the sickening details that it involves. I shall not attempt to lead you into that dreadful field, but I make this appeal to you. I do hope that every one of you will for himself and herself endeavour, in such a degree as your position may allow of you to endeavour, to acquire some acquaintance of them, because I know that when I say that a case of this kind puts exaggeration out of the question, I am making a very broad assertion which would in most cases be violent, which would in all ordinary cases be unwarrantable. But those who go through the process I have described, or even a limited portion of the process, will find that the words are not too strong for the occasion.

What witnesses ought we to call before us? I should be disposed to say that it matters very little what witness you call. So far as the character of the testimony you will receive is concerned the witnesses are all agreed. At the time that I have just spoken of, six or eight months ago, they were private witnesses. Since that time, although we have not seen the detailed documents of public authority, yet we know that all the broader statements which have been made up to that time and which have made the blood of the nation run cold have been confirmed and verified. They have not been overstated, not withdrawn, not qualified, not reduced, but confirmed in all their breadth, in all their horrible substance, in all their sickening details.

And here I may say that it is not merely European witnesses with whom we have to deal. We have American witnesses also in the field, and the testimony of the American witnesses is the same as that of the European; but it is of still greater importance, and for this reason – that everybody knows that America has no separate or sinister political interest of any kind in the affairs of the Levant. She comes into court perfectly honest and perfectly unsuspected, and that which she says possesses on that account a double weight.

Gladstone then reviewed the evidence presented in the vivid and incontrovertible article which Dillon had written for the *Contemporary Review* of August 1895. Dillon had (he said) travelled to the Ottoman empire 'laudably making use of a disguise for the purpose ... so that he might make himself thorough master of the facts'. What he found was later confirmed by the delegates of Britain, France and Russia. Gladstone's conclusion from reading Dillon's report was that 'we are not dealing at all with a common and ordinary question of abuses of government or the defects of them. We are dealing with something that goes far deeper, far wider, and that imposes upon us and upon you far heavier obligations'. He summed up the substance of Dillon's article in 'four awful words – plunder, murder, rape and torture.' For all the acts connoted by these words the Ottoman government was responsible, and the various parts of its executive had apparently joined in a 'deadly competition' as to which should prove most able at killing. Gladstone ridiculed the idea that the actions were reprisals for an Armenian insurrection. He then looked at the manner in which the authorities had received the reports of the killings:

Now these are the proceedings that took place in Armenia; the accounts of them, how are they received in Constantinople? You would have said that if there had been the smallest foundation for the sanguine hopes which were 40 years ago entertained of better government in Turkey, that they would have been received with the greatest eagerness to discover and punish the wrongdoers, the marauderers. On the contrary, they were received in the first place with denial. It was exactly the same with regard to Bulgaria in 1876. After those Bulgarian outrages, which were afterwards established by the authentic researches of the present Lord Cromer on the part of the English government, a formal statement was printed and circulated by the Turkish ambassador in this country – I have got a copy of it – himself, in the name of his government, denying entirely the Bulgarian outrages, saying that there were a few insubordinate people in Bulgaria whom it had been necessary to 'keep in order', but treating the whole thing as a falsehood. The fact is, that falsehood was the weapon which the Turkish government then used, and falsehood is a weapon familiar to its use. It was used on this occasion, but the powers were aware with whom they were dealing, and delegates on the part of France, England and Russia were appointed, you know. Although we have not seen the documents yet, we know that, speaking largely, they completely made good all the worst allegations that had been made. But these horrible outrages made known at Constantinople excited on the part of the Ottoman government no desire except the desire to cover them by falsehood, by fraud, by delay.

Gladstone believed that coercion was appropriate in Armenia, even though it was a concept which he held should usually be excluded from diplomacy. He made a careful linguistic distinction between the words 'must and 'ought'. (This was interesting, in that his detractors have considered him to have been verbose and linguistically insensitive.)

Recollect that grammar has something to do with these cases. Recollect that the word 'ought' sounding in Constantinople has no force, can have no weight or validity whatever attached to it. On the contrary, the pressure of the sister monosyllable, the word 'must' is perfectly understood, and it is a known fact supported by positive experience, which you can verify upon the map of Europe, that the permanent and judicious use of that word never fails in its effect.

In outlining his proposals for the future, he hinted that a status for Turkish Armenia, similar to that granted to Mount Lebanon in 1860–61, might be appropriate. He used the words 'local self-government', reminding his audience of its success elsewhere in Ottoman Turkey: here were 'experiments in a sense of justice'. He recalled Ottoman statesmen of an earlier time – 'if only men like Fuad Pasha and Ali Pasha who were in the government of Turkey after the Crimean War could be raised from the dead and could inspire the Ottoman policy with their spirit and their principles.'

He concluded his speech with these words:

> We must be careful to demand no more than what is just, but at least as much as is necessary. We must be determined that by the help of God, so far as depends upon us, that which is necessary and that which is just shall be done, whether there be resistance or whether there be none.[2]

One year later, after a winter of massacres of Armenians by the Ottoman authorities, and a particularly severe outbreak of official bloodshed in the Ottoman capital in August 1896, Gladstone spoke again, this time at Liverpool, before an audience of 6,000 people. The Earl of Derby, a Conservative, presided as lord mayor. The *Liverpool Daily Post* reported Gladstone's speech.

> It is true, ladies and gentlemen, that I have lived a long political life, and I have borne high and responsible office; but it is not in regard to either of these circumstances that I now come before you. I make no claim whatever to have authority in any shape. I come here as a loyal subject of her majesty and especially as having been admitted through the kindness of the local authority to call myself your fellow townsman as the possessor of the freedom of Liverpool. My lord mayor, it has been well said that we stand today on a higher platform than the platform of party. There is no man here, whatever his opinion on ordinary politics may be, who will scruple to own them or will appear as though he were ashamed of them. But the national platform on which we stand gives a higher claim and a greater authority to those sentiments which as I believe are universally entertained from one end of the country to the other; and my lord mayor, I will say for myself that as on this occasion it is a duty to renounce all party sympathies and party recollections, so it is a duty most easy to perform. I, for myself, entertain not only a lively hope, but a strong belief that when in the course of time we are made more largely acquainted with the inner relations of governments in the transactions of the last two years, we shall find that the present deplorable situation, to whatever it may be due, is not due either to the act or the default of the government of this great country.
>
> Now, my lord mayor, before I come to the resolution which I have undertaken to move, there are certain subjects which I should wish, if I may, to clear up. There are most important distinctions to be drawn in this matter, especially on the ground that the sufferers under the present misrule and under the horribly accumulated outrages of the last two years are our fellow Christians. But permit me to say, seconding that which has already been said, we do not prosecute the cause we have in hand upon the

ground that they are fellow Christians. This is no crusade against Mahomedanism. This is no declaration of an altered policy or sentiment as regards our Mahomedan fellow subjects in India. Nay more, I will say it is no declaration of universal condemnation of the Mahomedans of the Turkish empire. On the contrary, my lord mayor, amidst the dismal and heart-rending reports of which we have heard already, and have heard so much, one of the rare touches of comfort and relief has been when we have seen, in spite of the perpetration of massacre by agents of the government, in spite of the open countenance given to massacre by the highest authority, yet there have been good and generous Mahomedans who have resisted these misdeeds to the utmost of their power, and who have established for themselves a claim to our sympathy and to our admiration. Although it is true that these persons are Christians on whose behalf we are met, I confidently affirm, and you will back me out in affirmation, that if instead of being Christians they were themselves Mahomedans, Hindoos, Buddhists, Confucians, or what you like to call them, they would have had precisely the same claim upon us to that which has brought us here today, and it would have been incumbent upon us with the same force and the same sacredness that we recognise in it at the present moment.

There is another distinction, gentlemen, less conspicuous, that I would wish to draw your attention to. You have been discouraged by the attitude and by the tone of several of the continental governments. Do not too hastily assume that in that attitude and tone they are the favourable representatives of the people whom they rule. It has been well said that the ground upon which we are standing here is not British, is not European – it is human. And nothing narrower than humanity can pretend for a moment justly to represent it. Now, my lord mayor, it may have occurred to some that the atrocities, which it is hardly possible to exaggerate, have been boldly denied; and we are told by the government of Turkey that the destruction of life is not the work either of the sultan or of his agents, but is the work of revolutionists and agitators. In answer to this, we may say that we don't rely on the reports of revolutionists or agitators. We rely on the responsible reports of our own public men. Nay more: while we know that there are those among the six powers who have shown every disposition to treat the case of the sultan with all the leniency and all the friendship that they could, yet every one of them concurs in the statements upon which we stand, and in giving an entire denial to the counter statements of the Turkish government. There is here an illustration which may be of some value and convenience. This is not the first time that we have been discussing horrible outrages perpetrated in Turkey, and perpetrated not by Mahometan fanaticism but by the deliberate policy of a government. The very same thing happened in 1876 ...

After drawing a comparison with the Bulgarian atrocities, Gladstone turned his attention to the recent events. With ironic hesitation he placed responsibility for the massacres upon the head of the sultan himself.

They presented to the sultan a truly formidable document in which they announced that such proceedings as these must really cease. And why must they cease? Because if they continued they would create a prejudice against the Turkish government and against the sultan. A prejudice was the result to which they were to lead. I ask you to put yourselves into the position of the guilty author of these massacres. Be he who he may, don't you think that remonstrances like this serve the purpose of inciting him to proceed? What more does he want if you confine yourselves to a paper war? A paper war is that which alone is necessary for the execution of his purpose, and that paper war conveys to him all that he wants – namely the assurance of impunity.

My lord mayor, and ladies and gentlemen, in speaking upon the subject at Chester 15 months ago, I said that there was an opinion abroad that extermination was the true object of this policy, and I said that it was an opinion so monstrous in itself and so difficult of execution that I was not prepared to give my belief, my adherence, to that idea that such purpose could be entertained. I must say that, so far as the Armenians are concerned, that idea is far less irrational than it was 15 months ago. The sultan has added massacre to massacre; he has paraded massacre under the eyes of the representatives of every court in Europe. He remains unpunished and intact, and boldly asserts his innocence and his merit ...

All that has been done to the present time has been done with the concert of Europe, and we ought to consider what that concert is. It is a powerful, an august, and in many cases a most useful instrument for good. But its successes have not been uniform, and I should be disposed to take upon the whole a less favourable view of its application to the eastern question than was taken by one of the speakers who preceded me, and with whose remarks I so cordially agree. I think that usually the concert of Europe has failed in what is known as the eastern question. Good has been done by the concert of Europe – aye, enormous good. These eyes of mine have witnessed the events which have liberated from 15 to 20 million of the subject races from the domination of Turkey. But how has that been effected? Greece has been constituted, and subsists and flourishes, but Greece was not constituted by the concert of Europe ... The liberation of Bulgaria, and the liberation of the sister states around it, was not due to the concert of Europe ... It was by other action, and by sole action, that that great and beneficial change was brought about which has converted the territories of the Balkan peninsula – speaking in the main and generally – from a land of servitude into a land of freedom.

Things however changed after 1878, and Gladstone deepened his criticism of the European powers: 'Collectively, the powers have undergone miserable disgrace.'

How could Britain extricate herself, and gain the power for moral action? Gladstone had always believed in united action by the European powers, so this was for him a bitter moment. But with a magnificent grasp of what needed to be done, he jettisoned his belief in a common European policy. Britain should not separate itself completely from Europe: duty does not permit that we 'should place ourselves in a condition of war with united Europe, or should take measures which would plunge Europe generally into a state of war.' So how far should Britain go it alone?

> I entirely deny that that means that England is under all circumstances to abandon and forgo her own right of ultimate judgement upon her own duties, her own powers and her own opportunities, and to make herself a slave to be dragged at the chariot wheels of other powers of Europe ... While I admit that it is of the utmost importance that we should study every means of consulting the sentiments of other powers, and of carrying them along with us, I do not believe that the way to carry them along with us is to show a servile determination under all circumstances, and whatever they may decide, to make their consciences beforehand the measure of our own.

After looking at the history of the Ottoman 'reform' since the Crimean War, Gladstone put forward his ideas for appropriate policies: that the British ambassador should be recalled from Constantinople, and that the powers should, in seeking a solution to the problem of the situation in Armenia, issue a self-denying ordinance whereby they would agree not to seek any individual advantage from the situation. He recalled that such a pact had been made by Britain and France at the beginning of the Crimean War, and had been honourably kept. Gladstone's peroration to this, almost his final speech, in which he spoke for one hour and thirteen minutes, was as follows:

> Come what may, let us extract ourselves from an ambiguous position. Let us have nothing to do with countenancing; let us renounce and condemn neutrality; and let us present ourselves to her majesty's ministers promising them in good faith our ungrudging, our enthusiastic support in every effort which they may make to express by word and by deed our detestation of acts not yet, perhaps, having reached their consummation, but which have already come to such a magnitude and to such a depth of atrocity that they constitute the most terrible, most monstrous series of proceedings that have ever been recorded in the dismal and deplorable history of human crime.[3]

*The Liverpool Daily Post* gave a pleasing, if a trifle sentimental, account of Gladstone's departure from Liverpool and return to Hawarden. Beneath the headline 'The Return to Hawarden: Mr Gladstone Gratified', its anonymous reporter wrote:

Mr Gladstone, looking hale and hearty, full to the brim of the enthusiasm he had displayed at Hengler's Cirque, arrived at the James Street station amid the plaudits of an immense throng. Nothing could exceed the cordiality with which he was received by all classes and conditions of the population. Women waved their pocket-handkerchiefs, and men doffed their hats and sent them spinning round in sweeping circles through the air, while the whole atmosphere was rent with plaudits, such as can only be heard when a great popular hero is in the midst of the people whom he loves, and by whom he is loved in return. All sectional differences were submerged into the one great idea of the hour, so that it might be questionable if the grand old hermit of Hawarden in his lifetime received such universal tokens of public approval as were manifested yesterday. He was temporarily the end-all and the be-all of the city from the lowest to the highest rung, the acclaim with which he was greeted being the swelling volume of a mighty host of admirers, embracing all ranks from the humble cotton-porter to the lordly merchant and shipowner.

The crowd at James Street station was immense and Mr Gladstone and party disappeared from view amid a perfect tornado of applause. Chief Superintendent Hassall was on duty in front of the station premises, and had some difficulty in keeping the crowd back, but it was only for a moment, for the spectators were all well behaved and deeply interested in the whole tenor of the proceedings. Once inside the station, perfect comfort was secured, though the huzzahs of the roaring crowd penetrated right away down into the tunnel shaft.

When the distinguished party left the train at James Street station to journey to Hengler's Cirque the carriages in which they had travelled from Hawarden were drawn along to the Central (low-level) station. While the ceremonial proceedings at the Town Hall were being brought to a conclusion, the special train was brought back to the James Street station, directly opposite the gate leading to the platform ... The train was a few minutes late in starting, but this was not attributable in any way to the railway officials, who displayed throughout a punctiliousness which could only be compared to the procedure observable on the occasion of a royal progress. On getting settled down in a saloon carriage, Mr Gladstone appeared to be somewhat overcome, but it was apparently more the weight of his thoughts than physical fatigue. He remained for a considerable time buried in thought, giving no attention to anything or anyone about him. Meantime, Mrs Gladstone was reclining on a sofa, being to all appearances considerably fatigued by the day's proceedings.

The journey to Hawarden was accomplished in about an hour, the train bowling along in the most pleasant manner. At the wayside stations a number of working men put in an appearance, and even from the fields adjoining the railway the labourers and farmers gave every token of interest in Mr Gladstone's latest campaign. At Hawarden station Mr Gladstone took leave of the railway officials, whom he cordially thanked for the excellent arrangements which had been made for the comfort of his party. Two carriages were in waiting to convey the guests to the castle, one with a cockaded footman and driver, the other a one-horse 'shay' after the heart of Oliver Wendell Holmes. Mr Gladstone chose the humbler vehicle for himself, while Mrs Gladstone and Mrs Drew drove off in the other. The rest of the members of the family, who were all good walkers, proceeded to the castle on foot.

Mr Gladstone did not conceal his satisfaction with the journey to Liverpool. The weather, as a whole, was brilliant, though a heavy shower fell as the train was nearing Connah's Quay. 'We've had a pleasant day, a pleasant journey, and a good meeting,' he observed. Mr Gladstone was in excellent spirits, and quite lively in his movements, on reaching Hawarden. He changed from one carriage to another with great agility, to suit the convenience of Mrs Gladstone. Questioned with reference to the general impression of Mr Gladstone as to the position taken up by Liverpool on the Armenian question, Mr Herbert Gladstone said his father was greatly pleased. There was a most impressive tone to the whole deportment of the people, whether at the meeting or in the streets. With regard to Mr Gladstone's health, it was stated that he had felt no injurious reaction whatever from his great exertions ... The party returned to the castle amid the respectful salutations of the villagers, who were naturally anxious to learn how the great Liverpool demonstration had gone off. The shades of night darkened down soon afterwards round the heights of Hawarden, though far out along the stretches of the Dee there was an aureole of light, gleaming like the new-born hope of Armenia.[4]

## THE DUKE OF ARGYLL

Another strong advocate of the cause of the Armenians at this time was George Douglas Campbell, 8th Duke of Argyll (1823–1900), who was sometimes known as the 'radical duke'. He had been a member of Palmerston's Crimean War cabinet. At that time he had taken the view that the fate of Turkey should 'not rest in the hands of Russia, but might be decided by Europe'. Argyll had quarrelled with Gladstone over Ireland, but the Armenian issue brought them together in 1895.

In 1896 he published a powerful critique of the stance of the British government towards Ottoman Turkey, entitled *Our Responsibilities for Turkey:*

*Facts and Memories of Forty Years.* This short work is lucid, terse and epigrammatic, and informed with political scepticism and a powerful moral sense. It is an elaboration of the background which had led Gladstone to his conclusion on the Ottoman question. At this time, a moral position in relations between governments was more acceptable than it is today. Politics was seen – as indeed were art and poetry – to be closer to religion and morality than is now the case. Britain held that it had a right to criticize Turkey – a role which can now only be accomplished by a non-governmental organization such as Amnesty International. This right was however not entirely conjured out of the air, but derived in this instance from a clause in the treaty of Paris, which had concluded the Crimean War, in which it was made clear that Ottoman Turkey was being admitted to the comity of nations on condition that it reformed its administration.

The Duke of Argyll's book, unfashionable today (you will not find it named as a required text for the study of Middle Eastern affairs), is compelling reading. The author begins by claiming that the British people have 'a consciousness of some heavy responsibility' in the recent Armenian massacres. Argyll's purpose is to give to that awareness focus and articulation. The main direction of British policy since the Crimean War had been one of 'protecting Turkey, with a view to the repulse of Russia from an exclusive and dangerous domination over the east of Europe'. This policy went back to Pitt's call to parliament, during the Ochakov crisis of 1791, to arm against Russia, a summons which had proved unpopular and rapidly faded. Edmund Burke and Charles James Fox had both spoken against it, Fox memorably exclaiming, 'It was new to the British House of Commons to hear the greatness of Russia represented as an object of dread.' (Twenty years earlier England had helped create the Russian fleet.) Yet, if an anti-Russian stance had been unpopular in 1791, from the time of the overthrow of Napoleon, the fickle British grew decidedly opposed to Russia. Only occasionally did public opinion change course, and government policy almost never. Briefly Britain collaborated with Russia in the destruction of the Turkish fleet in 1827, a momentous event in the Greek War of Independence; but the following year Navarino received Wellington's memorable designation: an 'untoward event'.

Thenceforward British hostility to Russia became a central aspect of policy, fed by Russian gains in the north Caucasus and Central Asia, and by the arrogant manner in which Russia claimed the right to be the sole arbiter of the fate of Ottoman Turkey. Britain held that the empire's fate should rather be the concern of all the powers. The Crimean War was internationalized by the destruction of the Ottoman fleet by that of Russia at Sinope in 1853. Argyll pointed out that a larger proportion of the fleet survived than had at Navarino; yet the event roused British public sentiment to a perfect fury. In the war itself Ottoman Turkey was rescued from domination by Russia.

After the Crimean War, Britain was left 'foremost as a nation in joint responsibility – by irrevocable deeds and by definite transactions – for the very existence of the Turkish government as a power even pretending to independence'. Ottoman Turkey was also admitted to participate in the advantages of the public law of Europe. Instead of being left like one of the Central Asian or Caucasian emirates or khanates, as doomed vassals of imperial Russia, Turkey was granted a full measure of independent existence. In keeping with this new status, Turkey was asked by the powers to proclaim an edict (known as the Khatt-i Sherif of Gulkhane), recognizing the fundamental principles of European civilization, and extending to all classes of her subjects some security for life, religion, property and honour. The edict was an intimation that Turkey, acknow-ledged for the first time to be a negotiating equal with the European powers, was expected, in matters of internal government, to behave approximately as they did. The edict was incorporated into the treaty which concluded the Crimean War.

How much change was there twenty years later?

One word sums up the whole result of Turkish promises: – Nothing. Perhaps we ought to have expected this. It is the inevitable tendency of all bad things, when freed from restraints, to go from bad to worse ... Our consular agents at such places as Erzeroum and Trebizond reported to us, from year to year, the continued infamy of the government, the misery of the people, and the increasing desolation of the country. The Mussulman peasantry did not escape oppression. But the full force of it fell, of course, on the Christian population. Their lives, their property, and the honour of their families, were all at the mercy of an organized system of villainy.[5]

Argyll was critical of his political allies: 'All I can say is that in 1867 I found mere party Liberalism to be as dead in conscience and as apathetic on our duties in the east as the most fossil Toryism.' As regards the Eastern Crisis of 1875–78, he pointed out that the public antipathy to Turkey, and diplomatic odium that Constantinople was receiving, and even the warning that Britain would not now save her from invasion – all this derived not from committing an external aggression, 'but that government had proved itself so incorrigibly bad that it could no longer be endured'.[6]

Analysing the failure of the 1856 joint guarantee put forward by the powers for the reform of Ottoman Turkey, Argyll declared crisply: 'What was everybody's business was nobody's business, and twenty-two years' experience had proved that this miscellaneous protectorate was quite useless for the professed purpose.'[7]

The treaty of Berlin (1878) gave to Russia the protection of the Christian populations of the Ottoman empire – all except one. That was the Armenians. Here, 'we insisted on reverting to the principles of the treaty of Paris, which substituted a European for a Russian protectorate'. These had proved impossible to implement in eastern Europe. They would be still more impossible to implement in Asia.

Britain's special responsibility lay in its separate treaty with Turkey, known as the Cyprus Convention, in which Britain undertook to defend Asiatic Turkey (that is, Turkish Armenia and neighbouring lands) against Russia, in return for a lease on Cyprus, and a guarantee of reforms in Armenia. 'No security was asked or offered for the execution of these promises.'[8] Britain had learnt nothing since the systematic evasion of reform which had occurred since 1856. The machinery of Ottoman government remained, in the words of Sir Fenwick Williams (who, as Argyll reminded us, had fought as Turkey's ally in 1854–55), 'an instrument of oppression unequalled in the world'.[9]

And so we have gone on for fifteen more years since 1880, failing to take, or even to attempt taking, any effectual measures to protect the helpless populations subject to a government which we know to be so cruel and oppressive – populations towards whom we lay under so many respons-ibilities, from our persistent protection of their oppressors...

Then let us put 'that and that' together. Let us remember that this is not a government with which we have had nothing to do, or for which we have no responsibility, but a government which the European powers, and we especially, have been protecting and nursing for half a century – saving it from its natural enemies – surrounding it with artificial privileges and immunities, and tightening its grip over its subject populations, only salving our conscience by continuous scolding which we knew to be futile – and then we may indeed begin to think, with remorse and shame, of our handiwork, and of its results.[10]

Argyll ended with a prescription for what had to be done.

But as the past is now irrevocable so far as the destruction of human life, and the desolation of a whole country, are concerned, it becomes our special business to note the causes which have led up to this catastrophe, and have placed us in a position so distressing and so humiliating. We must change our course. We must shake off the abominable doctrine that these holocausts of human victims are but the necessary price to be paid for a policy essential to our national interests ... Let us recollect that every human life among the thousands which have been sacrificed in Armenia – which we could have saved by any exertion on our part – and which we have not saved because of the doctrine I have traced, has been nothing less than a human sacrifice on our part to our fetish god of the 'Balance of Power' in Europe or in Asia ... The very first thing we must do is to clear ourselves of the guilt of any more identification of Turkish rule, and of its horrible concomitants, with the maintenance of our interests in the east.[11]

The activities of Argyll and others like him did have some limited effect. Britain ended its close identification with Ottoman Turkey. Lord Salisbury moved the centre of British interests in the Near East from Constantinople to Cairo, and never again did Britain extend support towards Ottoman Turkey.

## G. N. CURZON

During 1895–98, the under-secretary of state for foreign affairs in Lord Salisbury's administration was George Nathaniel Curzon (later Lord Curzon), traveller, intellectual, and from 1898 to 1905 Viceroy of India. He put the government's viewpoint on Armenia when the subject was debated in the House of Commons on 3 March 1896. His forthright speech is remarkable for two reasons: it represented the views of a Conservative and Unionist government, which was and is usually held to favour Turkey for regional reasons; and also because Curzon himself was a man of unrivalled world view, with a broad understanding of Britain's true imperial needs, and precise knowledge of the position of Russia vis-à-vis India. The whole debate is worth reading. Here are extracts from Curzon's speech. The 'member for Sheffield', Sir Ellis Ashmead-Bartlett, was well known for his pro-Turkish views, and for his propensity to deny that the Ottoman government ever acted other than in a manner both gentle and progressive.

> I will not pursue the Sasun incident; it is as dead as are its unhappy victims. But any impartial observer reading that Blue-book [that is, the diplomatic correspondence relative to the events published by the government] must come to the conclusion that, with only the slightest provocation and the meanest excuse, a campaign of extermination was carried on by Kurds and Turks against the defenceless population of that mountainous district, and that, if the number of those killed can only be counted in hundreds, the number must be estimated at many thousands of those who suffered misery and destitution as bad as death itself ...[12]
>
> Before I finish, I wish to say a few words about the massacres [of September–December 1895]. If it had not been for the speech of my hon. friend the member for Sheffield (Sir E. Ashmead-Bartlett) I do not think I should have been tempted to say anything about them. I think my hon. friend has not succeeded in giving the House a fair impression of the nature of those massacres. I do not see how it is possible to deny or even

to minimize the appalling character of the events. I suppose I have read more about them than any other man in the House, because, in addition to the papers in the Blue-books, I have had other information, public and private, put before me, and my impression of the massacres is this. There are certain common characteristics that may be traced in the history of all these events. They all occurred posterior to the granting of reforms in Constantinople, which in itself suggests some connection with that step. They occurred almost simultaneously in widely scattered parts of Asia Minor. They were begun in most cases by the Turks. I regard the countercharge, though true in a few instances, as having broken down in the great majority of cases. The massacres were openly participated in by Turkish soldiers and gendarmes. The proceedings were conducted with an organization that was perfect and almost mathematical. The massacres in some cases began and ended by sound of trumpet. The Armenians were almost the only Christians who suffered. The lives of other Christians were spared, and the number of Turks killed was quite insignificant. And finally these massacres were followed by the forcible conversion of the survivors to Mahommedanism, accompanied by the greatest cruelty.

I do not care to dispute with my hon. friend on this side of the House as to the actual number of the slain. The number of 25,000 has been given on the authority of the delegates of the six embassies at Constantinople; and further, the evidence on which they reported was evidence derived from their consuls on the spot – as well as from eye-witnesses, missionaries, priests, travellers, and others – and figures are only given where the data for a correct estimate existed, and many of the districts are omitted altogether. I myself believe that the number of 25,000, instead of being a maximum, is rather a minimum.

It is also fair to bear in mind the incidents that have followed this carnival of blood. Whole districts have been desolated; whole villages have been destroyed. Thousands of persons are at the present moment wandering about in the cold mountain districts of Asia Minor, homeless, penniless, foodless, and capable of absorbing every penny of the tens of thousands of pounds that you can send them. I do say deliberately, seeing that this has been challenged in this House – and I am only repeating what has been said by others of greater responsibility than myself – that this is one of the most appalling stories of misery that I have ever read. If the poet's saying is true that 'mortal tears to mortal woes are due,' I cannot imagine a more pathetic spectacle in history.[13]

## WILLIAM WATSON

The poet William Watson wrote with urgency and passion on the Armenian situation of the mid 1890s. Sir William Watson lived from 1858 to 1935; he was knighted in 1917. A minor poet, he holds the distinction of having been passed over for the Poet Laureateship in 1895 in favour of Alfred Austin, on account of his strongly held views on Armenia, which were at variance with British government policy.

The events stirred Watson to write energetically in favour of the persecuted people, against the tyranny of the sultan, and to be highly critical of his own government's refusal to act.

Watson held that morality was primary in international affairs. 'Abdul the Damned on his infernal throne' was perhaps his most famous line. If there was wickedness in the east, it was, he believed, the British empire's job to sort it out. He cared little for the complexity of Anglo–Ottoman relations. To him there could be no ambiguity in Britain's international moral stance. His views on the sultan were said to have caused some dismay at the Foreign Office, which tended to favour the line taken by Wellington and Palmerston.

As literature, Watson's poetical language was not original or arresting. Although described as 'post-Tennysonian', he could never have written anything with the questing force of Tennyson's *Ulysses* or *Tithonus*. His verse lacks an inner life. Nevertheless, there is a somewhat primitive strength to some of his lines, and he does not deserve the total obscurity into which he has fallen.

In 1896 he published a sonnet sequence about Armenia, entitled *The Purple East*. (The title was taken from Shelley.) It was published by John Lane, and its frontispiece was engraved by G. F. Watts. Watson had been writing verses critical of British policy on Armenia throughout 1895, which Salisbury and Balfour would have noticed. Nevertheless, in London's literary circles he was the front runner for the laureateship throughout much of 1895. *The Spectator* backed him, as did a group of writers in *The Idler* of April 1895. However, politics counted for more than versification, and Alfred Austin, the high Tory, was duly chosen at the end of December. Austin took the line that it was 'best to be patient' on the matter of Ottoman Turkey and Armenians.

Watson followed *The Purple East* with another volume of poems entitled *The Year of Shame*. Here he re-worked some of the earlier verses and added others. The Bishop of Hereford wrote a foreword, as if to emphasize the ethical nature of the contents. If anything, this second collection was more outspoken.

From *The Purple East*, this sonnet is entitled 'The Plague of Apathy'.

No tears are left: we have quickly spent that store.
Indifference like a dewless night has come.
From wintry sea to sea the land lies numb
With palsy of the spirit stricken sore,

The land lies numb from iron shore to shore.
The unconcerned, they flourish; loud are some,
And without shame. The multitude stand dumb.
The England that we vaunted is no more.
Only the witling's sneer, the worldling's smile,
The weakling's tremors, fail him not who fain
Would rouse to noble deed. And all the while,
A homeless people, in their mortal pain,
Toward one far and famous ocean isle
Stretch hands of prayer, and stretch those hands in vain.[14]

One of the poems in *The Purple East* is entitled 'If' – a rare example of a title being shared by two poems. Watson's 'If' makes a point on public policy and morality: that if a nation desired to, but was unable to, intervene in a calamitous situation such as the massacres, then that nation was unfortunate. '*But if ye could but would not*' – the emphasis was Watson's – what then would be the ultimate verdict on that nation?

Watson's poem on Gladstone, calling upon him to make the brave and outspoken statement that he went on to make at both Chester and Liverpool, is perhaps the strongest of the set. In its 1896 appearance it was entitled 'The Tired Lion'. Some ten years earlier Watson had written a sonnet in opposition to Gladstone's imperialistic policy in the Sudan.

Speak once again, with that great note of thine,
Hero withdrawn from Senates and their sound
Unto thy home by Cambria's northern bound, –
Speak once again, and wake a world supine.
Not always, not in all things, was it mine
To follow where thou led'st: but who hath found
Another man so shod with fire, so crowned
With thunder, and so armed with wrath divine?
Lift up thy voice once more. The nation's heart
Is cold as Anatolia's mountain snows.
O, from these alien paths of dire repose
Call back thy England, ere thou too depart –
Ere, on some secret mission, thou too start
With silent footsteps, whither no man knows.[15]

'Whither no man knows': one cannot help feeling that here was also a curiously appropriate summation of his country's policy towards Armenia.

# CHAPTER 10

# *The Key of Truth*
## *F. C. Conybeare and Armenian Studies*

F. C. Conybeare (1856–1924) pioneered Armenian scholarship in England. He was educated at Tonbridge School and University College, Oxford, where he obtained a double first in classical languages, philosophy and ancient history. He was then elected a fellow of the college; but, benefiting from a private income, and finding the round of college business somewhat unchallenging, he resigned, and on the advice of the great orientalist D. S. Margoliouth devoted himself to the study of the Armenian language. Later he took up Georgian too. Initially he studied for the purpose of textual criticism of the Greek classics. But in the course of his studies he grew interested in Armenian history and language for their own sakes. On his second visit to Armenia, in 1891, one of the monks of Echmiadzin showed him a manuscript which had been copied in 1782, entitled *Banali Chshmartutian* ('The Key of Truth'). This was perhaps the sole surviving manuscript of the Armenian protestant dissenters known as the eastern Paulicians, who may or may not have been the same as the Tondraketsi: the sectaries whom Gibbon had described in chapter 54 of his great work. Conybeare is best remembered today for his edition and translation of this text of early Armenian spiritual dissent.

Conybeare was far from being a dry scholar. He expressed his opinions on matters touching beyond his sphere of scholarship with a passion unusual in a linguistic specialist of his date. His first venture into controversy was to give strong support to Alfred Dreyfus against the anti-Semitic French establishment; in 1898 he published a book entitled *The Dreyfus Case*. ('The actions of the French War Office have outraged the conscience of the civilized world.') In the second place, his study of Christian origins appears to have led him to a position of religious scepticism, articulated in a book published in 1909 with the title *Myth, Magic and Morals: a Study of Christian Origins*. This is an exercise in comparative religion based largely on textual criticism of the bible. Despite its scepticism, it was written with charity: 'We must not scoff at anything in which our fellow beings have found refuge from elemental terrors.' It stands somewhere alongside *The Golden Bough* and *Totem and Taboo*.

His third deed of dissent was to declare, in 1914, that responsibility for the outbreak of the first world war lay squarely with H. H. Asquith and Sir Edward Grey. This unpopular opinion, which was made public in spite of his wishes, led to much ill-feeling, and he was attacked in the British press. Sentiment in Oxford seems to have been strongly against him, and he left north Oxford in 1917 to live in Folkestone for the rest of his life. In his will he generously donated his Armenian books and pamphlets to the London Library.

His extensive scholarly work started with a *Collation with the Armenian Versions of the Greek Text of Aristotle's Categories, &c.* (1892). In 1898 he published his version of the highly important Paulician text, *The Key of Truth*, and in 1905 produced a translation of some of the earliest Armenian rites (but not the eucharist). He compiled the catalogues of Armenian manuscripts for both the British Museum (1913) and the Bodleian Library (1918), and wrote the articles on 'Armenian Church' and 'Armenian Language and Literature' for the eleventh edition of the *Encyclopedia Britannica*. He also contributed extensively to journals. A complete bibliography of his work can be found in the *Revue des études armeniennes* for 1926.

From his edition of *The Key of Truth*, here he remarks on some stylistic points of this revelatory protestant text.

The prayers in it remain pure and limpid examples of classical speech; and it is natural that they should have most successfully resisted the vulgarizing influence of centuries of rude and untaught copyists. They seem to me to be older than the controversial chapters which accompany them, and to belong to the fourth or fifth century. He who considers in what form an English book, written in the tongue of the ninth century and transmitted almost ever since entirely by copyists who were ignorant and persecuted peasants, would have come down to the present age, has a right to pass judgement on *The Key of Truth*. The history of the sect as we read it fills us with just wonder that their book is not tenfold more corrupt and vulgarized than it is. There is constantly in it the hand of some eloquent and earnest writer, who knew how to pen clear, bold, nervous, freely flowing and unembarrassed paragraphs, when, to judge by the works of Gregory of Narek and Gregory Magistros, the Armenian church writers were about to reach the lowest level of obscurity and affectation, of turgid pomposity and involution of phrase.

On the whole, therefore, the evidence of the style is in favour of, and not against an early date. But when we consider the contents we are obliged to refer the book to the ninth century at latest. The exordium is unmistakably from the pen of some great leader and missionary of the

Paulician church. Mark the words: 'I have spared nothing to give unto you, my new-born children of the universal and apostolic church of our Lord Jesus Christ, the holy milk, whereby ye may be nourished in the faith.' He has been inspired by the Holy Spirit to reveal 'the way, the truth and the life' to those from whom till now the truth had been hidden by pedantry and deceit. He will with The Key of Truth open 'the door of truth,' long since shut upon his flock by Satan. This exordium, almost Pauline in its mixture of tenderness and authority, bespeaks some great missionary and restorer of religion in Armenia. We have also hints of cruel persecutions and vicissitudes which had too long delayed the appearance of a manual, to the composition of which 'love of the truth of our Lord and zeal for the Holy Ghost, and the urgent entreaties of many believers had long since impelled him.' At last, in response to the entreaties of many believers, and urged by supreme necessity, he has thrown aside all other interests of this transitory life in order to compose this humble and unpretentious book, which they are nevertheless to read and ponder unto the glory of Jesus Christ their mediator.[1]

Conybeare identifies the great teacher as Smbat Bagratuni, who was born in the late eighth century and ruled over Taron (the region of Moush today) from about 856. He marvels at the sect's ten-century history of silently endured spiritual dissent, and hypothesizes that 'it is probable that in the present day many of the converts of the American Protestant missions in Erzeroum, Mush, Bitlis, Kharput and other places are Paulicians by heredity.'[2] The Englishman seeks to set the record straight for the dissenters. 'Eastern Christianity,' he says, 'Greek and Armenian alike, is to this day bleeding from the wounds which, in its persecutions of these early Puritans, it inflicted on itself.'[3] For at almost the same time as they were enduring harsh persecutions, so too was Alp Arslan laying waste Greater Armenia. The object of Conybeare's especial wrath was Gregory Magistros, who had been appointed duke of Mesopotamia by Byzantine emperor Constantine Monomachos (1042–54), on condition that he crush the Paulicians. Conybeare saw him as a turgid self-justifier. To the scholar, his linguistic insensitivity was an integral part of his persecuting personality.

From the translation of *The Key of Truth*, this passage summarizes the sect's understanding of Jesus' baptism. Conybeare reminds us that adult baptism only was permitted, performed at around the age of thirty. A child was given a name at eight days; and later in life the spiritually privileged might, by the laying on of hands, enter the ranks of the elect. Baptism remained the central event for the majority.

> So then it was in the season of his maturity that he received baptism; then it was that he received authority, received the high-priesthood, received the

kingdom and the office of chief shepherd. Moreover, he was then chosen, then he won lordship, then he became resplendent, then he was strengthened, then he was revered, then he was appointed to guard us, then he was glorified, then he was praised, then he was made glad, then he was pleased, and then he rejoiced. Nay more. It was then he became chief of beings heavenly and earthly, then he became light of the world, then he became the way, the truth and the life. Then he became the door of heaven, then he became the rock impregnable at the gate of hell; then he became the foundation of our faith; then he became saviour of us sinners; then he was filled with the godhead; then he was sealed, then anointed; then he was called by the voice, then he became the loved one, then he came to be loved by angels, then to be the lamb without blemish. Furthermore he then put on the primal raiment of light, which Adam lost in the garden. Then accordingly it was that he was invited by the spirit of God to converse with the heavenly father; yea, then also was he ordained king of beings in heaven and on earth and under the earth ...[4]

The following prayer was said during the rite of election:

I thank thee and magnify thee, heavenly father, true God, who didst glorify thine only-born son with thy holy spirit. Also the holy universal and apostolic church of thine only-born son didst thou adorn with divers graces. And now adoring, we pray thee, merciful father, send on this thy newly elected one thine infinite grace; that coming it may fill him and be to him a rampart and armour against thine adversary, who for ever and continually desires to ensnare those who have believed on thine only-born. Now therefore, lay thy holy right hand upon thy servant here elected, and keep him from evil and from temptation of the world by the intercession of thy true son, now and for ever and to eternity of eternities. Amen.[5]

## CHAPTER 11

# 'To Strengthen an Ancient Church'
# The Anglican and Armenian Churches

Cordial relations developed between the Armenian Church and the Church of England in the Victorian era, for several reasons. In the first place, both churches were national churches, which at the same time considered themselves to be part of the universal church. In the second place, the Anglican Church did not seek to make converts from the Armenian Church, unlike the missionaries of the American denominations, or the Church of Rome. And in the third place, the sympathy which Gladstone and others showed for the plight of Christian communities under the yoke of the Ottoman empire was understood by Armenians to have Anglican Christianity as its main moral driving force.

An educational mission of the Anglican Church to the Assyrian Christians, whose historic land today traverses the border between Turkey and Iraq, was established in 1877. It set forth its aims in the following admirably non-imperialist manner: 'Our object in sending out these two priests is not to bring over these Christians to communion of the Church of England, nor to alter their ecclesiastical customs and traditions, nor to change any doctrines held by them which are not contrary to that faith which the Holy Spirit has taught as necessary to be believed by all Christians, but to encourage them in bettering their religious condition, and to strengthen an ancient church.'[1]

There had been informal and fairly imprecise contacts between the Anglican and the Armenian churches even earlier, since soon after the treaty of Paris. Certain Armenian clergymen appear to have been instrumental in encouraging relations between the two churches. One was Bishop Megrdich Shahmanian from Aintab. He was the driving force behind the Armenian Anglican United Church, founded in 1857, and by 1882 reported by the British consul to have 'several hundred families' in and around Cilicia as members. Bishop Megrdich and his followers liked the Anglican prayer-book. Might he have been a descendant of a Paulician family, one of those whom Conybeare mentioned? It is possible, but only remotely so. Aintab was not a dissenting stronghold.

Another Armenian clergyman who forged links with the Anglican Church was Garabed Stepanian, from Diyarbakir. He was ordained priest by Bishop Samuel Gobat in Jerusalem in 1862. But the problems of Anglophile Armenians were considerable. In the first place, defecting clergy incurred the strong displeasure of the hierarchy of their own church, and sometimes of the community as a whole, and in the second place, the Ottoman state put many obstacles in the way of setting up a new church.

In 1881, following an approach from the Armenian Church to the see of Canterbury, an Armenian Educational Association was established in Constantinople. Then, in 1892, representatives of the Armenian Church again contacted the Anglican Church, seeking organizational help for the Armenian Catholicosate of Cilicia (which at this time was more usually known as the Patriarchate of Sis). Letters were exchanged, and in the early months of 1892 two Anglican clergymen, the Revd. William Everingham and the Revd. Charles Robinson, travelled to Cilicia to survey the situation. This is the main substance of the report produced by the Revd. Robinson, which is dated 29 April 1892. The text has been slightly edited in places.

My Lord Bishop [Salisbury],

I am sending herewith a report of a visit to the Catholicos of Sis and to the Armenian Church within his patriarchate. The visit was paid by the request of the committee of which your lordship is chairman, in consequence of the reception of a letter by his grace the Archbishop of Canterbury from the Catholicos of Sis, signed by the principal bishops and priests throughout the patriarchate in which an earnest appeal to the Church of England was made to afford to the Armenian Church similar assistance towards educating their candidates for the priesthood to that which had already been given to the Assyrian Church. The object of my visit was to report to the committee on the possibility and desirability of an effort being made to accede to this request.

The Patriarchate of Sis includes within its jurisdiction Cilicia, Cappadocia and parts of northern Syria and Mesopotamia: it contains eight dioceses presided over by bishops, viz. Adana, Furnuz, Hadjin, Malatia, Mandgalek, Sis and Yozgat, in addition to the above there are many dioceses placed under the charge of vartabeds (of whom there are twenty in all) who are not in episcopal orders, the number of priests in the Patriarchate is about 250.

After visiting the Armenian Patriarchate of Jerusalem and ascertaining the efforts which have recently been made to improve the standard of education in the large Armenian monastery situated there, I went to Adana, where I met the Catholicos, and presented to him the letters from the Archbishop of Canterbury and Bishop Blyth of Jerusalem together with the letter from your Lordship. After spending two days with the Catholicos I commenced a ride of 800 miles through the Patriarchate of Sis (during the first week of which I was accompanied by the Revd. Wm. Everingham who came out with me from England and was the joint bearer of the letters to the Catholicos) in order to interview as many as possible of the bishops and vartabeds who had signed the letter to the Archbishop of Canterbury, and to ascertain by personal investigation the condition and the special needs of the Armenian Church at the present time.

In presenting this report I would desire to draw the especial attention of the committee to the following points.

i) The need which exists for raising the standard of education of candidates for the Armenian priesthood.

ii) The desire on the part of the Armenians to supply such need.

iii) The nature of the help for which an appeal has been made to the Church of England.

iv) The location and cost of maintenance of a theological school, such as it has been proposed to establish.

v) The political difficulties connected with the establishment of the same.

I. In regard to the first of the above points, it seems scarcely possible to overestimate the greatness of the need which exists for raising the standard of education at present required from candidates from [i.e. for] the Armenian priesthood. Nearly seventy per cent of the Armenian priests are unable to preach at all, and of the remaining number comparatively few ever attempt to do so, or to give any instruction at all to the people under their charge. Many of them are barely able to read and write, and some of them do not even understand the liturgy which they use, owing to the ignorance of the *krapar* (i.e. the ancient Armenian language), in which both the liturgy and the bible are written. In many places the people are beginning to demand that sermons should be preached at least occasionally, and in consequence of the inability of their priests to comply with this demand, many of the better educated laity are constantly tempted to desert their ancient church in order to obtain from the Presbyterian and Congregationalist missionaries who are working among them, the religious teaching which they have vainly sought from their own duly ordained clergy. In some districts moreover, owing to the unwillingness of the bishops to ordain ignorant and unsuitable men, the greatest difficulty is experienced in supplying the demand for priests ...

II. As far as it has been possible to judge from the opinions expressed by a large number of bishops, priests and laity, I believe that the desire to raise the standard of education is both widespread and real. The Church of England is in fact generally regarded by the Armenians as the only branch off the Catholic Church which would be willing to afford the help so greatly needed, without at the same time endeavouring to make proselytes from the Armenian Church. This conviction has been strengthened by the knowledge of what the Church of England has recently done on behalf of the ancient Church of Assyria.

III. In regard to the nature of the help for which the Armenian Church has appealed, it is desired to establish a theological school in which candidates for the priesthood, monks (from the number of whom the bishops are chosen) and teachers might be educated. The only school within the Patriarchate of Sis which attempts to fulfil such a purpose is that in the monastery at Sis – at present entirely inadequate to supply the needs of the whole patriarchate. At Etchmiadzin there is a school containing 150 students, but it is impossible that this school should supply the needs of the lower province, where Turkish is universally required.

IV. The question as to the location of the school is seriously complicated by difficulties of a political nature.

The only sites which appear in any way possible and which have been suggested by the authorities of the Armenian Church are a) Sis in Cilicia, b) Marash in Cappadocia, and c) Nicosia in Cyprus.

In favour of Sis it may be urged:

i) That Sis is the seat of the Catholicos, and has been so for many centuries;

ii) It possesses an ancient monastery, in which a school containing about 20 students is now held, which would become the nucleus of the proposed theological school.

On the other hand it may be stated:

i) The climate of Sis is so unhealthy that it is impossible to keep teachers or students here for more than half the year, moreover no satisfactory drinking water can be obtained during any part of the year.

ii) The monastery is in a most ruinous condition, and it would require a considerable sum of money to render it possible for a theological school to be held here even during the winter months.

iii) Though the population of Sis during the winter is about 5000, half of whom are Armenian Christians, none of the people either speak or understand the Armenian language, Turkish being the only language used.

iv) Political difficulties seem to render the establishment of a school there little short of impossible.

In favour of Marash it may be urged

i) The climate of the town is excellent;

ii) There are 15,000 Christians in the town who speak the Armenian language;

iii) The priests and laity in Marash are exceedingly anxious that the school should be established here. There are moreover 700 children under instruction in the Armenian schools in Marash.

[Points iv and v relate to the cost of the project, and the condition of the buildings; and there follows a section on arguments for and against siting the school in Nicosia]

The political difficulties arise from the extreme dislike and jealousy shown by the Turkish government towards her Armenian subjects. As a result of my visit to the school in the monastery at Sis, the Pasha sent to arrest the native Armenian teachers of the same. One of them succeeded in escaping, the other two were thrown into prison, solely on the ground of their having been seen conversing with an Englishman. The bishop of Zeitun and 40 of his people are at present, and have been for months past, in prison in Aleppo, in consequence of a political disturbance which took place at Zeitun, in which there is every reason to believe the bishop had no concern whatever.

Efforts are being made by the government to close the existing Armenian schools and so to prevent Christian children from obtaining any religious instruction or any secular education other than that which is given in a Mohammedan school. The greatest possible pressure is being brought to bear, too often successfully, to compel the Christians to become Mohammedans. The oppression under which the Armenian Church is suffering is such that it is extremely doubtful as to whether permission could be obtained from the government for the opening of a school, or whether if obtained, it would not be rendered useless by the restrictions which would be placed on students.

Conclusion

Should the political difficulties prove surmountable, I would earnestly recommend that an effort be made to assist the Catholics and the authorities of the Armenian Church to establish a Divinity School in Marash, as there is every reason to believe that if the Church of England should for the next few years assist in the establishment and maintenance of such, the benefit would be out of all proportion to the money spent or the effort made.

Charles Henry Robinson[2]

The cost was estimated at £400–500 per annum for the first two years; after which the project would be self-supporting. But nothing came about, almost certainly because the 'political difficulties' did not 'prove surmountable'. Anti-Armenian sentiment hardened within the Ottoman empire, coinciding with the sultan's ideological commitment to pan-Islamic policies, and his formation of the 'Hamidiye' cavalry from among the Kurdish tribes – a cavalry which was almost exclusively employed to harass and oppress the unarmed Armenian peasantry. In the circumstances, within the Armenian community, the priorities changed from seeking to develop schools and education, to the mere survival of the people amid a reign of terror.

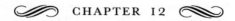

## CHAPTER 12

# 'At the Moon's Inn'
# Isabella Bird and Lucy Garnett

ISABELLA BIRD

Isabella Bird (Mrs Isabella L. Bishop, 1831–1904) was a spirited traveller, who showed qualities of enterprise and energy not often found among women of her generation and background. Before her journey to the Islamic Orient she had travelled to Japan, the Rocky Mountains and the Hawaiian Archipelago. In 1890 she travelled to Persia and Kurdistan, and John Murray published her account in the following year. She was awarded an honorary fellowship of the Royal Scottish Geographical Society. In further travels she visited Tibet and China. From each of her journeys she produced a book.

Much of *Journeys in Persia and Kurdistan* is distinguished by its unbiased observation. At that time, observers of the Islamic empires were apt to use them as vehicles for a display of personal feelings unrelated to the living conditions of the people who inhabited the lands. In much of her writing Isabella Bird looked fairly and objectively at the people of the east, and recorded what she saw, leaving most of her own attitudes out of the picture.

She stayed a month in New Julfa, and found it 'clean and comfortable'.

It is a 'city of waters'. Streams taken from a higher level of the [river] Zainderud glide down nearly all its lanes, shaded by pollard mulberries, ash, elm, and the 'sparrow-tongue' willow, which makes the best fire-wood, and being 'planted by the river of waters', grows so fast that it bears lopping annually, and besides affording fuel, supplies the twigs which are used for roofing such rooms as are not arched.[1]

The houses, some of which are more than three centuries old, are built of mud bricks, the roofs are usually arched, and the walls are from three to five feet thick. All possess courtyards and vineyards, and gardens into which channels are led from the streams in the streets. These streams serve other purposes: continually a group of Armenian women may be seen washing their clothes in them, while others are drinking or drawing water just below. The lanes are about twenty feet wide and have narrow rough causeways on both sides of the water channel. It is difficult on horseback to pass a foot passenger without touching him in some of them.

Great picturesqueness is given in these leafy lanes by the companies of Armenian women in bright red dresses and pure white robes, slowly walking through them at all hours of daylight, visions of bright eyes and rosy cheeks. I have never yet seen a soiled white robe! Long blank mud walls, low gateways, an occasional row of mean shops, open porches of churches, dim and cool, and an occasional European on foot or horseback, and groups of male Armenians, whose dress so closely approaches the European as to be without interest, and black-robed priests gliding to the churches, are all that is usually to be seen. It sounds dull, perhaps.

Many of the houses of the rich Armenians, some of which are now let to Europeans, are extremely beautiful inside, and even those occupied by the poorer classes, in which a single lofty room can be rented for twopence a week, are very pretty and appropriate. But no evidence of wealth is permitted to be seen from the outside ...[2]

They were not allowed to have bells in their churches, (at Easter I wish they had none still), but now the Egglesiah Wang (the great church) has a fine campanile over 100 feet in its inner court. The ancient mode of announcing the hours of worship is still affectionately adhered to, however. It consists of drumming with a mallet on a board hanging from two posts, and successfully breaks the sleep of the neighbourhood for the daily service which begins before daylight.[3]

The Armenian merchants have, like the Europeans, their offices in Isfahan. The rest of the people get their living by the making and selling of wine, keeping small shops, making watches and jewellery, carpentering, in which they are very skilful, and market-gardening; they are thrifty and industrious, and there is very little real poverty ... The Armenian women are capital housewives and very industrious. In these warm evenings the poorer women sit outside their houses in groups knitting. The knitting of socks is a great industry, and a woman can earn 4s [20p] a month by it, which is enough to live on.[4]

From the empire of the Qajar Persians, Isabella Bird travelled north-west into that of the Ottoman Turks. From Bitlis, she wrote on 10 November 1890: 'I arrived here two days ago, having ridden the 90 miles from Van in three and a half days ... the early winter weather is absolutely perfect for travelling.'

The first day's half march ended at Angugh, an Armenian village on the river Hashal on the plain of Haidzar [Hayotsdsor: 'Armenian valley'] ... the views are magnificent en route, especially of the Christian village of

Artemid, on a spur on a height, with a Moslem village in gardens below, with green natural lawns sloping to the lake. At Angugh I was well accommodated in a granary on a roof, and as there was no room for my bed, found a comfortable substitute in a blanket spread upon the wheat. The next day's march was through exquisitely beautiful scenery, partly skirting deep bays on paths cut in the rock above them, among oaks and ferns, and partly crossing high steep promontories which jut out into the lake. A few villages, where strips of level ground and water for irrigation can be obtained, are passed, and among them the village of Vastan, the 'seat of government' for the district, and a Turkish telegraph station, but in the eleventh century the residence of the Armenian royal family of Ardzruni.

Art aids nature, and there are grand old monasteries on promontories, and Kurdish castles on heights, and flashing streams and booming torrents are bridged by picturesque pointed arches. There are 150 monasteries in the region, and the towers of St George at the mountain village of Narek, high on a rocky spur above one of the most beautiful of the many wooded valleys which descend upon the lake of Van, lend an air of medieval romance to a scene as fair as nature can make it. Nearly all the romantic valleys opening on the lake are adorned with one or more villages, with houses tier above tier in their rocky clefts, and terrace below terrace of exquisite cultivation below, of the vivid velvety green of winter wheat. These terraces often 'hang' above green sward and noble walnut trees. Occasionally the villages are built at the feet of the mountains, on small plateaux above steep-sided bays, and are embosomed in trees glowing with colour, from canary-yellow to crimson and madder-red, and mountains, snow-crested and forest-skirted, tower over all. Lake Van, bluer than the blue heavens, with its huge volcanic heights – Sipan Dagh, Nimrud Dagh, and Varak Dagh, and their outlying ranges – its deep green bays and quiet wooded inlets; its islets, some like the Bass Rock, others monastery-covered; its pure green shadows and violet depths; its heavy boats with their V-shaped sails; and its auburn oak-covered slopes, adds its own enchantment, and all is fair as fair can be.[5]

Isabella Bird's account of the Armenian peasantry has a convincing earthiness about it – an essence of unadorned existence and tenacity; and the qualities of character, and aspects of life of the Armenian peasant which she describes have a certain inner splendour to them (if only in their refusal to budge), whatever sophisticated urban woman or man may think 100 years later.

The Christians who, in this part of Kurdistan [north-west of Lake Van], are all Armenian by race, live chiefly on the plains and in the lower folds of the hills, and are engaged in pastoral and agricultural pursuits. My letters have given a faithful representation of them as dwelling with their animals in dark semi-subterranean hovels. The men are industrious, thrifty, clannish, domestic, and not given to vices, except that of intoxication, when they have the means and the opportunity, and the women are hardworking and chaste. Both sexes are dirty, hardy, avaricious, and superstitious, and ages of wrong have developed in them some of the usual faults of oppressed Oriental peoples. They cling desperately to their historic church, which is represented among the peasants by priests scarcely less ignorant than themselves. Their bishops constitute their only aristocracy.[6]

They are grossly ignorant, and of the world which lies outside the sandjak [district] in which they live they know nothing. The sultan is to them a splendid myth, to whom they owe and are ready to pay a loyal allegiance. Government is represented to them by the tax-gatherer and his brutalities. Of justice, the most priceless product of good government, they know nothing but that it is a marketable commodity. With the Armenian trading communities of the cities they have slender communication, and little except nationality and religion in common.

As a rule they live in villages by themselves, which cluster round churches, more or less distinguishable from the surrounding hovels, but there are also mixed villages in which Turks and Armenians live side by side, and in these cases they get on fairly well together, though they instinctively dislike each other, and the Turk despises his neighbour both for his race and creed. The Armenians have not complained of being maltreated by the Turkish peasants, and had there been any cause for complaint it would certainly have reached my ears.[7]

Finally, here is Isabella Bird's brief description of the Sanassarian College in Erzerum, a fine Armenian educational institution which, by an irony of history, was 29 years later to be the venue for the Erzerum Congress, which launched Mustafa Kemal's Turkish Nationalist movement.

One of the most interesting sights in Erzerum is the Sanassarian College, founded and handsomely endowed by the liberality of an Armenian merchant. The fine buildings are of the best construction, and are admirably suited for educational purposes, and the equipments are of the latest and most complete description. The education and the moral and intellectual training are of a very high type, and the personal influence of the three directors, who were educated in Germany and England, altogether 'makes for righteousness'. The graduation course is nine years. The students, numbering 120, wear a uniform, and there is no distinction of class among them. They are, almost without exception, manly, earnest, and studious, and are full of enthusiasm and esprit de corps. Much may be hoped for in the future from the admirable moral training and thorough education given in this college, which is one of the few bright spots in Armenia.[8]

## LUCY GARNETT

Lucy M. J. Garnett (who died in 1934) lived abroad all her life. She is the author of a two-volume study of *The Women of Turkey* (1890–91), and of *Greek Folk Poetry and Prose* (1896, also in two volumes). Her 1904 book, *Turkish Life in Town and Country*, contains important details about the condition and organization of the Ottoman empire. Like Isabella Bird, most of her writing is objective and factual; she keeps any prejudices to herself, and does not impose her attitudes on her readers. Although she was fascinated by the east, she was not overwhelmed by it, and was not swayed by magical projections of her own feelings.

Lucy Garnett's valuable account of the houses typical of the Armenians is also a mirror of the structure of the Armenian community itself.

The Armenians, besides constituting the bulk of the population in Armenia proper, form large communities in Constantinople and Adrianople, at Broussa and Smyrna [today respectively Istanbul, Edirne, Bursa and Izmir], and are also found in several of the smaller towns of Turkey. In the capital and at Smyrna the wealthier members of the Armenian communities are much more advanced in every respect than elsewhere, but in the latter city their adoption of Western manners and education dates even further back than in the capital. Here, as elsewhere, the Armenians occupy a separate quarter of the town, which compares favourably both as to the width and cleanliness of its streets and the architecture of its houses with the other quarters of the city, not excepting even that occupied by the so-called 'Franks', or Europeans.

Substantial proof of the comparative freedom from Muslim molestation now generally enjoyed by the subject races inhabiting the seaport towns, as compared with their position at the beginning of the last century, is afforded by the difference in style of houses of the better class built during the past twenty or thirty years. The older houses are externally somewhat gloomy in appearance, having often on the ground floor no windows over-looking the street, and the great double gateways are faced with iron and defended inside with heavy bars. The interior, however, even of these older houses, is the reverse of gloomy, for the spacious marble-paved entrance hall, furnished as a sitting-room, is divided only by a glass partition from a pleasant garden, and into this all the ground-floor rooms open. The upper stories far overhang the street, and in the narrow thoroughfares, as in the streets of old London, one can almost from the windows shake hands with opposite neighbours. This style of architecture presented many advantages when the dwellings of Christians were exposed to the attacks of the insolent and lawless Janissaries, though it did not always effectually protect their occupants from violence.

The modern houses, both large and small, are much more cheerful in appearance. The wide doorways, being above instead of below the level of the street, as in the older houses, are approached by handsome steps of white marble, and the spacious hall within is paved with large slabs of the same material. In the smaller houses – in Smyrna often of one storey only, on account of the frequent earthquakes – the drawing-room windows alone overlook the street, all the other rooms receiving their light and air from the hall. The far end of this apartment, which is used as a general sitting-room, often contains a fountain, and is converted into a species of conservatory with creepers and choice shrubs in vases. The rest of it is furnished with a Turkish sofa, a few common chairs, and in winter, a carpet. This, however, is but a middle-class dwelling. The abode of a wealthy Armenian is a palatial edifice, replete with European comforts and luxuries. Oranges, lemons and pomegranate trees blossom and bear fruit in their gardens, which are also fragrant with flowers all the year round. On the broad, raised footpaths, tessellated into graceful patterns with black and white pebbles, saunter the almond-eyed Mariems and Taquis in loose oriental garments and with slipshod feet, or in the latest fashions from Paris, according to circumstances and the time of day. The beautifully situated village of Buyukdere on the Bosphorus is a favourite resort of the wealthy Armenians of the capital, many of whom pass the summer months in the elegant marine villas, which, rising behind each other up the steep hill, command a magnificent view of the wonderful waterway and its picturesque banks.

The dwellings of the poorest class of Armenians – the hamals, or porters, and the boatmen and fishermen – though small, are not, as a rule, without a certain amount of decent comfort, suited to their mode of life. There is very little, if any, overcrowding among either the Christian or Muslim poor of Turkey, each family having its own separate cottage, generally approached by a little courtyard; and the exclusiveness of Oriental family life renders any sub-letting to lodgers extremely rare.

The houses in Armenia Proper present a striking contrast to those above depicted. The traveller visiting these remote regions at the present day finds the inhabitants of the Armenian villages living in houses precisely similar to those described by the great Greek general Xenophon, in his 'Retreat of the Ten Thousand'. These dwellings now, as then, are mere burrows in the ground; the front is formed by terracing the slope of a hillside for the space of a few yards, the room or rooms are excavated in the hill, and all the soil dug out is thrown against the side walls and on the roof, which is supported by strong wooden posts and beams. In some of the towns – Erzerum for instance, which is situated on the lower slopes of a mountain – the style of building is very similar. Each room is built like a separate house, with a flat roof which communicates with those above and below it by means of steps. One may walk along these terraces from house to house, over a great part of the town, and when stopped by a street, a moderate leap will suffice to clear the chasm, so narrow are the thoroughfares. The space of ground occupied by a rich man's house is consequently enormous, and the top, on which grass grows luxuriantly, looks like a terraced field. On the broad, mushroom-shaped chimneys the storks build their nests unmolested year after year, winging their way to warmer climes at the approach of winter, and greeted by the children on their return with glad sounds of welcome. During the brief hot season the family live briefly on the housetop, and the whole family frequently bring up their mattresses and cushions, and sleep 'at the moon's inn' in company with their many domestic pets.

The floors of all these houses are below the level of the roadway. A low, wide door gives access to a dark central passage, on one side of which is the ox-stable, or byre, and on the other are the kitchen, store-room, and private apartments of the family. Each room has a rude stone fireplace, in which are burnt cakes of tezek, a fuel made from the sweepings of the byre, largely used throughout Asia Minor. Some of the wealthier houses may boast a few chairs and tables; but, as a rule, the furniture consists of a low, wide sofa round three sides of the room, covered with beautiful stuffs of native manufacture, and some valuable Persian or Kurdish rugs spread over the thick carpet of home-made grey felt which covers the floor. The walls are whitewashed, and the wooden ceilings are curiously carved and painted ...

The byre is the most curious part of an Armenian house. It sometimes contains scores of cattle, whose animal heat greatly contributes, during the long winter months, to the warmth of their human neighbours. One end of this room is occupied by a railed-in platform, used by the men of the family as a reception-room for male visitors. It is furnished with the customary divan and rugs, and on the walls and ceiling are suspended saddles, bridals, guns, pistols and other weapons of war or the chase, while underneath the floor the dogs of the household have their abode ...

A great many curious ceremonies are observed by the Armenians in connection with such family events as births, marriages, and deaths. A wedding takes a whole week to celebrate, and when a wealthy farmer dies all the inhabitants of the village are publicly invited by the priest in church to the funeral feast. They have also retained a great many strange superstitious practices, and believe in the existence of a variety of supernatural beings possessing propensities and powers both benevolent and malevolent. In the long winter nights, when the snow lies thick in the streets and on the housetops, the women fancy they hear in the howling of the wind the shouts and laughter of these tricksy beings. And the young women and girls, when the day's tasks are done, gather round the grandmother, who relates strange creepy stories of the pranks of the djinns, or charming romances dealing with peris, magicians and enchanted palaces, while the grandfather, sitting cross-legged in his fur-lined pelisse in the corner of the divan, tells the boys tales of the Armenian heroes of old.

Sitting in their open doorways in summer, and at their windows in winter, is a favourite pastime of the Armenian women of the seaboard cities, as, indeed, with all their Christian neighbours. This practice, which is perhaps seen to greatest advantage in Smyrna, offers a strange contrast to the usual rigidity of manners observed in the east. For though custom forbids the young women to receive the visits of acquaintances of the other sex in the house save on special occasions, it allows them in the afternoons to hold levees at the windows, and during the carnival this licence is by many extended to the evenings, when gay parties of the *jeunesse dorée* of this Asiatic capital roam the streets in disguise, giving notice of their approach by music, or merely by beating the primitive doubana – an earthen jar with a piece of parchment tied over the opening. The windows of the modern houses are about six feet above the street, and below them the masquers station themselves with offerings of flowers or bon-bons for the fair ones, who, with elbows supported on the cushioned window ledges, lean out above them, eager to discover their identity – no easy matter, unless the masquers choose to give some clue. Soon they pass on to mystify others, and are succeeded by fresh groups still more fantastic, whose costumes represent wild Turcomans from the interior, Greeks from the Islands, Arabs from Mecca, or wandering dervishes from Khorasan. Watching these wild figures in the dark, narrow oriental street, with its mysterious gateways and overhanging upper stories, it is not difficult to fancy oneself rather in the days of the great Harun el Rashid than in the twentieth century.[9]

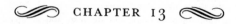

## CHAPTER 13

# 'A Vast Dome of Snow'
# H. F. B. Lynch

The outstanding British traveller to Armenia was without doubt H. F. B. Lynch (1863–1913), whose magnificent two-volume work *Armenia: Travels. and Studies* (London, 1901; reprinted 1965) is a monument to unwearying travel and deep study. Lynch was educated at Eton and Trinity College, Cambridge; his family appears to have combined public service and business. The firm of Lynch Brothers inaugurated a steamer service on the River Karun, Persia. Lynch himself was Liberal MP for Ripon in the parliament of 1906–10.

Lynch visited Armenia twice, in 1893–94, and 1898. His work has a unique breadth of style, which is combined with a typically late Victorian stress on scientific accuracy. The historical material is rich and thorough, and the author's appreciation of the aesthetic qualities of Armenian landscape and art show both vigour and a sense of inner repose. Here, Lynch is approaching Armenia from Georgia, and describes Mount Abul, which is situated just east of Akhalkalaki.

> Throughout the length and breadth of the Armenian highlands, themselves the loftiest section of the bridge of Asia between India and the Mediterranean Sea, there is perhaps no summit, with the possible exception of that of Ararat, which possesses a prospect at once so distant, so extensive and so full of interest as that which expands on every side from the triple peak of Abul. You stand on a stage which commands the fabric of the nearer Asia, without dwarfing the proportions of the majestic structure, without confusing the varied members of the vast design. The tableland with its open landscapes is unfolded before you, swelling and falling from plain to hummock, from hummock to rounded ridge, from vaulted ridge to the soaring arcs of an Alagoz and an Ararat, crowned with perpetual snow. The troubled outlines of the border ranges encircle the mysterious scene; and, far away, from a gloomy background to this full sunlight and radiant atmosphere, lurid flashes are reflected through layers of murky vapour by the snows of Caucasus, infinitely high.[1]

Later, Lynch and his companions – a cousin, a Swiss mountaineer and a photographer – approached Yerevan (here as ever called Erivan), from Ashtarak in the north, a route familiar 70 years earlier to Yusuf and Hajji Baba.

By eleven o'clock we had procured horses and were again on the road to Erivan. The entire region is strewn with rocks and presents the same bleak appearance, except where, here and there, a stream descends the barren slopes and sustains a slender line of green. In such places you may discern the rare site of a village, a few poplars, the grouped architecture of a church. At length, after long winding between the stony eminences, we opened out a view over the whole plain. The sky had not yet cleared, and mists obscured the forms of the mountains; but the whole lap of the plain was revealed. Patches of soft blue relieved the surface of the dim country – the vegetation of the rich campagna about the banks of the Araxes. We rode on, always descending, over these stony uplands, until they dipped to the floor of the level ground. Luxuriant gardens filled the gently-pursing hollow, intensely green after the heavy rain of the preceding day. Pools of water lay on the road; the water-courses were brimming over. The orchards were clothed with fruit of ideal perfection in form and colour; we admired the size and brilliant hues of the clustering peaches, side by side with the bending branches of the apple and pear trees, with the deep shade of the walnut and the mulberry trees. Ripe grapes hung in abundance from the low vine stocks ... Such are the outskirts of Erivan, a town embowered in foliage.

Perhaps Lynch's finest description is that of Mount Ararat itself, which he climbed in 1893. Here is part of it:

There he stands, like some vast cathedral, on the floor of the open plain. The human quality of this natural structure cannot fail to impress the eye; and, although its proportions are not less gigantic than the opposite mass of Alagoz, it contrasts with the Cyclopean forms of that neighbouring mountain a subtle grace of feature and a harmonious symmetry of design. Slowly the long slope rises from the western distance, a gently undulating line; and, as it rises, the base gradually widens, advancing with almost imperceptible acclivity into the expanse of plain. So it continues, always rising against the sky-ground, always gathering at the base, until at a height of 13,500 feet it reaches the zone of perpetual snow. The summit region of Ararat presents the appearance of a vast dome of snow, crowning a long oval figure of which the axis is from north-west to south-east. The whole length of this roof, on its north–eastern side, is exposed to the valley of the Araxes. The vaulting is less pronounced upon the west than on the east, and ascends through a succession of snow-fields to the highest point of the dome ...

The extraordinary elevation of Ararat above the plain of the Araxes – it may be doubted whether there exists in the world another mountain which rises immediately from a level surface to such a height – is balanced and controlled by this broad and massive base, and by the exquisite proportions of the upper structure which rises to the snowy roof. Yet neither the strength nor the symmetry of this admirable fabric has been proof against decay. Momentous convulsions from within have completed the work of gradual corrosion, and have opened a wide breach in the very heart of the mountain, where it faces the river and the plain. From the snow-beds of a lofty cornice to the base at the gathering of the seams, the whole side of Ararat has been fractured and rent asunder; the standing portion overhangs the recess with steep walls, which spread within it perpetual gloom. Further east, just in advance of the saddle which divides the Ararats, a grassy hill of unwieldy shape and flat summit interrupts the basal slopes, and offers an isolated contrast to the symmetry of the neighbouring forms. The chasm of Akhury and the hill of Takjaltu are minor features in the structure of Ararat which are seen and recognized from afar.

But most of all, as we realize the vision, which in the noblest shapes of natural architecture, the dome and the pyramid, fills the immense length of the southern horizon and soars above the landscape of the plain, the essential unity of the vast edifice and the correspondence of the parts between themselves are imprinted on the mind. If Little Ararat, rising on the flank of the giant mountain, may recall, both in form and in position, the minaret which, beside the vault of a Byzantine temple, bears witness to a conflicting creed, this contrast is softened in the natural structure by the similarity of the processes which have produced the two neighbours, and by their intimate connection with one another as constituents in a single plan. In this respect they suggest a comparison to a stately ship at sea, with all the close weaving and interdependence of hull and masts and sails. In the harmony of a common system each supplements and continues the other, and what Great Ararat is to the western portion of the fabric Little Ararat is to that on the east. The long north-western slope of the larger mountain is answered on the south-east by the train which sweeps from the side of the smaller towards the mists of the Caspian Sea; and there is the same correspondence between the slopes which are contiguous as between those which are most remote. The steeper side of the greater Ararat is turned towards the needle form of the lesser; and, standing in the valley which divides the two mountains, it appears that the degree of inclination of either slope is in exactly inverse proportion to their size. This pleasing interplay between constancy in essential principles and diversity of form invests the long outline of the dual structure with a peculiar charm. The differing shapes repeat one another, and one base supports the whole.[3]

Approaching Ararat from Yerevan, Lynch recorded:

Away on our right the distant chain of the Ararat system was shadowed
in tints of opal and indigo upon a rich ground of orange and amber hues;
the sun sets behind those mountains, and it was touching with globe of red
fire the fantastic peaks of the range. About us the plain lay grey and dim,
and all the light and glory was in the western sky. In the south the misty
fabric of Ararat loomed more gigantic as night approached; ever higher,
before us, in the paling vault of heaven the dome and the pyramid rose.
As we neared the first station on the road to Aralykh, the village of
Aramzalu, it seemed as if the snowy roof of the mountain were suspended
in the sky above our heads, a cold and ghostly island, holding the last
glimmer of day.[4]

Volume Two of *Armenia: Travels and Studies* is devoted to Turkish Armenia
(today eastern Turkey, although it should be noted that Aralykh, of the
preceding paragraph, is known today as Aralik, in Turkey). Lynch explored
the crater of Nimrud Dagh, and visited many Armenian villages,
monasteries, churches and schools which are now ruins, or less than ruins.
He tested the chemical composition of Lake Van; and as he was sailing
from one of the islands in the lake to Van itself, he recorded the following:[5]

It was half-past twelve when we put off; the wind had dropped, and
scarcely enabled us to forge ahead. For several hours we lay becalmed on
the bosom of the lake, here at its widest, in full face of the murky chain
on the horizon, which was reflected in hues of burnished steel. Banks of
mist shrouded the landscape, especially in the west where the mass of
Nimrud seemed encircled by the sea. A pest of little midges covered our
clothes and blackened our papers; then a shower fell, and yet another, and
they disappeared. About four o'clock a nice breeze freshened, coming from
the shore of low hills to our left. It brought with it rain; but a little later
the sun triumphed and burst the canopy of clouds in the south and west.
A double rainbow of great brilliancy rose from that near shore, revealing
the site of a little village. Our head was pointed to the rock of Van, which,
at this distance, shows like an island, even without the assistance of mirage.
The long barrier of the Kurdish range declines in that direction, and gives
way to a less steep and less gloomy ridge; but that outline again rises on
the further side of the city, to culminate in a lofty parapet of saw-shaped
edge. Varag – such is the name of this mass – commands the bay in which
Van lies from behind a spacious interval of garden and field. In the
landscape it strikes the last note of the tumultuous theme which is suggested
by the mountains in the south – a final trumpet blast by which the
procession marches onwards to the Persian plains.

    In the opposite quarter, across the lake, and against the declining slope
of Sipan, the gardens of Adeljivas might just be seen in shades of grey.

Those of Artemid were more distinct – a stretch of softness and verdure along the summit of a low cliff of yellow substance near the foot of the black range. A fragment of rock thrown seawards from those mountains was identified as the isle of Aghtamar. But the site of Van engrossed us, surpassing our expectations, high as these were. The rock, which had appeared at a distance to be an island, projected almost into the waters from a background of plain and without visible connection on any side. Battlements crowned its horizontal outline; while at its foot and along the shore luscious foliage, touched by autumn, covered all the inequalities of the ground. From rock and garden, and from the vague detail of the middle distance the eye was led upwards to the stony slopes of Varag; a bed of cloud lay captive upon them; but the jagged parapet stood out from a clear sky. Here and there, stray fragments of vapour, flushed by the evening, floated outwards from the dense canopy over the mountains in the south. The veiled snowfields of the range were revealed in fitful glimpses of yellow, unnatural light ... We moored our vessel by the side of a cluster of similar craft at the so-called harbour, and took the direction in which the town was said to lie. It is surrounded by a walled enclosure, and nestles at the foot of the rock. Darkness had fallen as we passed down its silent streets, made more gloomy by the shadows from the cliff. The bark of dogs, the sad refrain of an eastern song were the only sounds which broke the stillness of the night. Then we entered a broad chaussée which stretches inland to the suburb of gardens which usurps the importance of the fortified town. There are situated the consulates of the European powers, and the residences of the principal citizens. Poplars of great height rose from the irrigated ground on either side of the road. Side lanes led away from this broad avenue into the park of trees. After a walk which seemed interminable, and which occupied no less than three hours, we arrived at the British consulate at half past nine o'clock.

Here Lynch is travelling in the mixed Armenian–Kurdish region of Bingol, west of Lake Van:

Next morning before eight we continued our journey, the temperature registering 14 degrees of frost. Mist still hung over the valley; but we soon were raised above it, again ascending to the table surface which borders the depression on either side. Full sunlight streamed upon the undulating snow-field, and was reflected in tiny rays from a thousand little crystals, placed, like diamonds, on the heads of encrusted flowers. It was, indeed, over the face of an immense block of elevated country that our course was directed for some little time. Here and there, especially in the north, it appeared to be broken by chains of mountain; but the closer you approached such an apparent barrier, the more it assumed the familiar features – the flat edges, and the fanciful castles with the Cyclopean walls.

At half-past nine we obtained a view of the Bingol Dagh itself, in the furthest horizon of the south. We stood at a level of 7130 feet.

At ten o'clock we turned off eastwards to the bed of mist suspended above the river, which lies in a deep trough. Following for awhile along the sides of the lofty cliffs which confine it, we admired the play of the vapours, wreathing like jets of steam. From the edge of the cliffs on either bank, the table surface of the higher levels was seen to stretch east and west, and back to the peaks of the Akh Dagh – a sheet of snow, only broken by the gorge ...

It has already been said that the valley of the Bingol Su, or Upper Araxes, offers an easy approach to the districts on the north. The river pierces a wintry region of the table surface, and traffic is carried along its bed. But some 2½ miles below the village of Mejitli it enters a deep and impassable gorge. You mount to the summit of the lofty precipices which overtower its serpentine course. Again in the saddle at half-past one, we reached this commanding eminence at a quarter-past two. Nor did we descend afresh into the trough of the stream, which proceeded to thread a chaos of mountains in the east.

The view from any point was one of savage beauty. By slow degrees the flat surface of the elevated plateau was becoming riven and broken up. You could still discern the level snow-fields, burying the stream in the south, and coming towards you on either bank. But the cloak of winter had not yet hidden the yellow grass on the adjacent slopes; while in the east the scene was changing to a wild landscape of hill and mountain, upon which the snow had not yet effected a hold. A few miles further these features increased in definition. The layers of lava gave place to hard limestones, forming peaks which had weathered a soft white. Masses of rock, of a hue which was green as the rust of copper, or red like that of iron, were exposed on the sides of the hills. From a foreground of tufted herbage, sown with yellow immortelles, we looked across this troubled region in which the river wound its way – a ribbon of changing colours, skirting the foot of sweeping hillsides or confined in narrow clefts of stupendous depth. In the far east we caught a glimpse of the snowy dome of the Koseh Dagh, which overlooks the plain of Alashkert.[6]

Lynch's final sentences sum up his homage to the landscape that had imbued his sentences with such power and poetry. He is comparing the effect on a traveller of the luxuriant and romantic scenery in the valley of Meiriman, around the Pontic Greek monastery of Sumelas, with that of the austere, spare beauty of the Armenian plateau, which he had recently and regretfully left.

The last stage will introduce him to one of the most remarkable valleys in this or any other land. He should endeavour to arrange his visit during his return homewards, when the features of the tableland, with their majesty of form but bareness of surface, are freshly graven upon his mind. The contrast to that landscape which he will find in the Vale of Meiriman is at once sudden and complete. Vegetation of bewildering beauty takes the place of grandeur of outline; and only the impressive scale upon which Nature has moulded her work in Asia remains constant to the end.[7]

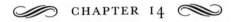

## CHAPTER 14

# 'Why Has the Tide of Civilization Paused?'
# Sir Edwin Pears and Noel Buxton

### SIR EDWIN PEARS

Sir Edwin Pears (1835–1919) was a barrister who practised in London until the age of 38, when a tenancy at the Constantinople bar became vacant, which he was able to take up. He rose to become one of the leaders of the British colony in the Ottoman capital. In the words of Arnold Toynbee, 'holding as he did, strong liberal convictions, he did not become imbued with that complacency towards the Turks – right or wrong – to which there has often been a tendency among western residents in the Levant, particularly in the British and French colonies since the Crimean War.'[1] Pears's book *Forty Years in Constantinople* is today considered essential reading for the study of the Ottoman constitutional revolution of 1908; and his *Life of Abdul Hamid* was recently reprinted by a New York publisher. This by contrast is not rated highly in Ottomanist circles, perhaps because it is too outspoken. Pears's book *Turkey and Its People* (1911) contains much interesting and original material on the nationalities of the Ottoman empire. Some of what he says on the Armenians tends towards the condescending and Eurocentric, and he uses the word 'race' where today we would not, since the word 'race' has become outdated, owing to the fact that it has no scientific or descriptive value. Yet much of this section of the book is illuminating, and gives a picture of a world which just four years later was to be entirely destroyed.

> In some respects the Armenians are the most interesting people in Asia Minor. They are physically a fine race. The men are usually tall, well built and powerful. The women have a healthy look about them which suggests good motherhood. They are an ancient people of the same Indo–European race as ourselves, speaking an allied language. During long centuries they held their own against Persians, Arabs, Turks and Kurds. Wherever they have had a fighting chance they proved their courage. In the economic struggle for life they and the Jews have managed to hold their own; but,

unlike the Jews, a large proportion have remained tillers of the soil. In commerce they are successful not only in Turkey, but in Russia, France, England, and India. Though subject to persecution for centuries under Moslem rule they have always, though sometimes after long and arduous struggle, managed to make their race respected. Notwithstanding a long series of massacres, in one of the latest of which, that under Abdul Hamid in 1894–97, probably at least 250,000 of them were killed or died from exposure, the race has continued to increase. A century and a half ago, the Armenian language was prohibited in several parts of Armenia. The penalty for speaking it was to have the tongue torn out. Nevertheless, Armenian is still almost everywhere spoken by the race. Its people are stiff-necked and have a toughness about them which prevents them being broken. They probably number about 4,000,000, of whom 2,000,000 are in Turkey, 1,500,000 in Russia, and the remainder dispersed throughout the world. They are thriving merchants in India and Persia, make splendid agricultural colonists in the United States, where they are already three or four considerable towns almost exclusively composed of them, and are found in almost every country in Europe.

Accepting Christianity at an early period their Church has always been jealous of outside interference. They keep their own rites and liturgy and only own obedience in religious matters to their own patriarch and catholicus.

Since the conquest of Constantinople by the Turks they have always been more open-minded than any other of the Christian races in the empire in reference to matters of religion ... While the Armenian is proud of his *millet* [religion-based nationality] and does not look kindly on a man who changes his religion, he does not consider that it should prevent him inquiring into the truth of other forms of Christianity, or adopting one of them if he likes. In the sixteenth century the Armenian church dignitaries corresponded with Erasmus and Melancthon and other reformers ...[2]

I believe the Armenian race to be the most artistic in Turkey. Many paint well and some have made a reputation in Russia and France. Amateur painting is so general as to suggest that the race has a natural taste for art. The picture gallery on the island of San Lazzaro at Venice, where (as also in Vienna) there is a convent of Armenian Catholics known from the founder as Mechitarists, contains many works of art by Armenians which won the approval of Ruskin. I can only judge of the Armenian love for music from the fact that nearly every family which can afford a piano has one upon which its members often play well, and that excellent choirs of Armenian singers come occasionally to the capital. Every observer notes that our best native companies of actors are Armenians.

Armenian and Greeks have furnished the brain of the Turkish empire during the last two centuries. Those who have known Turkey during the last thirty years will readily recall, not to mention living men, the names of a host of able public servants. Medical men, advocates, teachers, managing clerks, belonging to this race abound and have the confidence of natives and foreigners.

And yet this race, which in religion has never been aggressive, and which under Turkish rule only asked for the protection of life and property and desired to live at peace with its Moslem neighbours, was during the reign of Abdul Hamid so fiercely persecuted as to lead many to suppose an intention to exterminate all who belonged to it.[3]

NOEL BUXTON

Two years later, the Buxton brothers, Noel and Harold, travelled through Turkish and Russian Armenia, and published their impressions in 1914. Both were convinced Gladstonian Liberals. Noel (1869–1948) was MP for North Norfolk, and had helped to found the Balkan Committee in 1903. On the outbreak of the first world war he travelled semi-officially to the Balkans, to try to encourage eastern Europe towards the Allies; while in Bucharest he was shot through the jaw by a Young Turk. Harold (1880–1976), a deeply compassionate man, had entered the church. Before, during and after the war he was active in relief for those made destitute in the Balkans and the Caucasus.

*Travels and Politics in Armenia* is a valuable picture of conditions on the eve of the first world war. The book is not a masterpiece of organization; structurally it is quite confused. But in comparing the condition of Armenians living in the Russian empire with that of those living in the Turkish empire, it acts as an example for other works on Armenians. In a fine passage in the book, meditative and autumnal, which captures the essence of place and season as acutely as had Ker Porter 100 years earlier, Noel Buxton gives us a picture of Armenian life under the Romanovs, with glances across the border to that under the Ottomans.

One fine evening in September [1913] I took a drive from Erivan, the Russian town near Ararat, to see the Armenian villages of the Araxes valley. The plain, that would be arid waste without irrigation, has here come to look like the rich land one sees in Belgium from the Berlin express, small farms intersected with cypress-like Lombardy poplars, but here growing vines, rice and cotton. The presence of orchards – mulberry or peach – is denoted by high mud-walls along the road. As we moved farther the walls became continuous, and ripe apricots and quinces leaned over them. Water-courses lined our route on each side, feeding the roots of a double row of poplars. At intervals the wall was pierced by the windows of the farmer's house, flat-roofed, and at this season surmounted by stacks of corn. Old-fashioned mud-dwellings were yielding here and there to new fronts of stone, finely dressed. Big doorways at the side gave a glimpse of yards and verandahs, wellheads, great earthen jars, and farther on the orchard, with the raised wooden sleeping-platforms, used in the hot Araxes valley. In time the holdings become so thick as to give the effect of a continuous village, an unending community of picturesque market-gardeners – every man happy under his vine and his fig-tree.

As we travelled southward, and the sun sank westward, Ararat, flanked with sunset colour, dominated the world below. Ararat is higher than Mont Blanc, and standing alone it towers uniquely. Yet there is something specially restful about its broad shoulders of perpetual snow. With the soaring quality of Fuji it combines a sense of holding, up there, a place of repose:

> The high still dell
> Where the Muses dwell
> Fairest of all things fair.

In the shadow of the great mountain winnowers were using the last daylight on the green; a man was washing a horse after the burning day, standing shoulder-deep in the stream; buffaloes walked sedately home from their bath, shining like black velvet. The day's work was ending, and we now kept passing family groups sitting at the doorway. Here a boy was playing with a tame hawk; there a father, in most un-English fashion, held in his arms the baby.

The houses became continuous and shops appeared, wine-presses, forges, agricultural machines. Russian gendarmes gossiping outside the inn, wagon-builders and copper-pot makers. The slanting sun displayed a kaleidoscope of industry, not primitive and not capitalist – human economy at its most picturesque stage of development.

We halted to see the village priest, whose son was a student at St Petersburg University. As we sat in his balcony, the hum of village movement arose above the gathering stillness of nature, and we remarked on the prosperity of the priest's flock. He agreed; but there was a blot upon it – refugees from Turkey constantly arriving in rags, their property abandoned, driven out by violence and often by brutal violation, even of the very young. Russia was to them a godsend, though beggary was the price of escape from worse evil.

To the right of Ararat stretched the line of hills which forms the present Russo–Turkish frontier. Upon this horizon the sun set. It was a memorable combination – the eternal snow one associates with the north framed with the glowing brilliance of the southern sun. Byron was within the mark when he wrote of that sun:

> Not as in northern climes obscurely bright,
> But one unclouded blaze of living light.

There is something more than that. Those who have watched the white flames of a smelting furnace, and still more those who have climbed to its rim on a dark night, can picture something of the effulgence that streamed up from behind that blackening line of mountains – an effulgence quite correctly described as 'molten'. Hidden now from our view, it still bathed the hills from which these refugees had fled – that noble upland given over to misery and waste.

Why has the tide of civilization paused at that particular line of hills? The frontiers of Turkey on the European side were easily held against the small Balkan states, whose territories adjoined them, till those states became powerful by combination, but here the defence is obviously powerless. The fortifications of Erzerum itself have twice been in the hands of Turkey's great neighbour. Yet for thirty-five years the Russian armies have been as if paralysed. Forces even greater than they have said, 'Hands off that frontier, defenceless though it is.'

We are face to face with the Cyprus Convention and the Berlin treaty, which specify that this Turkish frontier is guaranteed by the powers, and by England in particular. Those documents, till you visit the spot, seem abstract and intangible embodiments of justice. Here they are concrete enough to the peasant escaping penniless through the hills; to the Armenian priest in Russia, trying to find him bread; to the Russian prefect, dealing with brigands who can always escape into a lawless country. These diplomatic instruments, usually cited as vague landmarks in past history, are here playing a tragically definite part.[4]

## CHAPTER 15

# 'Absolutely Premeditated and Systematic'
## H. H. Asquith, Lord Bryce and Arnold Toynbee

The first world war was a time of catastrophe for Armenians. The Young Turk party, in power in the Ottoman empire, took action to eliminate them from as many locations in Anatolia and Turkish Armenia as possible. The events were justified as a temporary wartime measure; but the destruction of women and children, and the killing of Armenians that occurred far from the war zone, show up such a justification as unconvincing, and tell us that the real intention was along the lines of racial mass-murder, or genocide. The appalling accounts told by survivors and eye-witnesses of mass-slaughter of civilians were naturally used by the Allies as war propaganda against the German–Turkish alliance. (Similar accounts of atrocity, perpetrated by the German army against Belgian civilians, had been used by the Allies earlier in the war as propaganda.) But the use of the accounts of atrocities as propaganda does not make them *ipso facto* untrue. Those who amassed details about the Ottoman atrocities on behalf of the Allied cause were too scrupulous and careful to accept any but the most objective and untainted evidence in preparing their case against the Young Turks.

During the war British leaders naturally made strong attacks on Germany's Ottoman allies, and used all available facts against them. In November 1916 the prime minister, H. H. Asquith, spoke thus in his Guildhall speech:

> I remember, years ago, acclaiming with premature and, as events have proved, ill-founded satisfaction the triumph of what was called the Young Turk movement over the spy-ridden and blood-stained tyranny of Abdul Hamid. We hoped in those days for the regeneration of the Ottoman empire from within. Our hopes have been falsified and frustrated, and I believe we all now realize that the continuance of Turkish rule in Europe, where the Turk has always been a stranger and an intruder, has already come to mean, and if it is allowed to persist will increasingly mean, that

the Turk is there only as a vassal and a subservient agent of German interest and ambitions.

Allow me to give you one practical illustration, and it is a very tragic one. Among the enslaved races who have suffered most from the Ottoman domination are the Armenians, the wholesale massacre of whom during the last two years has shocked the entire civilized and Christian world. In our own country, in Russia, and I believe even more in the United States of America, the incredible sufferings of this nation have aroused profound sympathy, and all three countries have raised large sums for their relief and their repatriation in the future. I need not say that his majesty's government look with profound sympathy on these efforts, and are resolved that after the war there shall be an era of liberty and redemption for this ancient people.[1]

About eighteen months earlier, on 28 July 1915, the British people had been first informed of the Armenian massacres. Some details of the events were given in a speech in the House of Lords by Viscount Bryce, the veteran supporter of the Armenians. He had asked the government spokesman for confirmation (if he could provide it) of the information that he had received of 'what is supposed to have been done in eastern Asia Minor, Armenia and elsewhere; but from what information has reached me I have little doubt that terrible massacres have been committed. This information comes partly from Tiflis, partly from Petrograd, and partly from Constantinople to Switzerland and Paris. The stories are that all through Armenia in the Taurus mountains and north-eastwards towards the Russian and Persian frontiers, and particularly in the districts of Zeitun, Moush, Diyarbekir and Bitlis, there have been extensive massacres ...'

According to my information there was, at Moush in particular, a very extensive massacre; at another place all the male population that could be seized were brought out and shot, and the women and children to the number of 9,000 were taken to the banks of the Tigris and thrown into the river and drowned. Similar horrors are reported from the other places ...

Replying for the government, the Marquis of Crewe, Lord President of the Council, said:

My Lords, I am grieved to say that the information in the possession of the Foreign Office on the subject which my noble friend has raised, although it is not much more ample than that of which he is already possessed, is in conformity with what he has told us. I fear that there can be no doubt that the general facts are as my noble friend has described them. The noble viscount and the most reverend Primate [the Archbishop of Canterbury] have reminded the House that some two months ago, in concert with the governments of France and Russia, representations were made in regard to the massacres which had been perpetrated up to that date, 24 May, to the effect that members of the Ottoman government and all their agents who could be shown to be actually implicated would be held personally responsible for the crimes that had taken place. Since then the crimes have increased in number and, if possible, in atrocity. Wholesale massacre and wholesale deportation have been carried out under the guise of enforced evacuation of particular villages, and there have been a series of other outrages such as my noble friend has described ... It is true, as has been stated by all the speakers, that for reasons quite obvious to anybody who follows the progress of the war that there are no immediate steps which we can take for the actual repression of these atrocities. All that we can do at the moment is to repeat, and repeat with emphasis, the expression of our determination, rendered more emphatic as the weeks go on and bring fresh evidence of these crimes, that those who can be held to be responsible for them, whether by their direct commission or by their inspiration – and all the more I am tempted to say the higher and the more responsible the positions they hold – should receive punishment accordingly.[2]

Just over two months later, on 6 October 1915, Lord Bryce gave the House of Lords further information about the nature and progress of the large-scale massacres of Armenians. Lord Cromer also participated in the exchanges; and the Marquis of Crewe again spoke for the government. The latter noted that details had reached London from the British consul in Batum, and he confined himself largely to the situation of Armenian refugees from the Ottoman empire who had fled to Transcaucasia.

Bryce rose to speak. His information came from missionaries, and from various Armenian sources. He confirmed that the number of 800,000 for those who had died was unfortunately 'quite a possible number'. This was because the proceedings 'have been so absolutely premeditated and systematic'. Orders came from the imperial capital, and those who refused to carry them out were dismissed. He described the procedure as follows.

The whole population of a town was cleared out, to begin with. Some of the men were thrown into prison; the rest of the men, with the women and children, were marched out of the town. When they had got some little distance they were separated, the men being taken to some place among the hills where the soldiers or the Kurds despatched them by shooting or bayoneting. The women and children and older men were sent off under convoy of the lowest kind of soldiers – many of them drawn from gaols – to their distant destination, which was sometimes one of the unhealthy districts in the centre of Asia Minor, but more frequently the large desert east of Aleppo, in the direction of the Euphrates. They were driven by the soldiers day after day; many fell by the way and many died of hunger. No provisions were given them by the Turkish government, and they were robbed of everything they possessed, and in many cases the women were stripped naked and made to travel on in that condition. Many of the women went mad and threw away their children, being unable to carry them farther. The caravan route was marked by a line of corpses, and comparatively few seem to have arrived at the destination which was stated for them. I have had circumstantial accounts which bear every internal evidence of being veracious, and I was told by a friend who lately came home from Constantinople – he belongs to a neutral country – that he had heard many accounts in Constantinople, and that what had struck him was the comparative moderation with which there atrocities were detailed by those who had first-hand knowledge of them.

To give your lordships one instance of the systematic way in which these massacres were carried out, it may suffice to refer to the case of Trebizond, a case vouched for by the Italian consul [Signor Gorrini] who was present when the slaughter was carried out, his country not having then declared war against Turkey. Orders came from Constantinople that all the Armenian Christians were to be killed. Many of the Muslims tried to save their Christian neighbours and offered them shelter in their houses, but the Turkish authorities were implacable. Obeying the orders which they had received, they hunted out all the Christians, gathered them together, and drove them down the streets of Trebizond past the fortress, to the edge of the sea. There they were all put out on sailing boats, carried out some distance on the Black Sea, and there thrown overboard and drowned. The whole Armenian population of from 8,000 to 10,000 was destroyed in that way in one afternoon.

Bryce emphasized that Islamic extremism had no part to play in the events, though leading Muslims did not intervene. Nor had there been any insurrection on the part of the Armenians. Armenian volunteers had fought in the volunteer regiments which had been formed in Trans-caucasia; but the vast majority of them were Armenians from the Russian empire. The Ottoman government had no excuse for its anti-Armenian policy. It seemed to be simply carrying out the maxim of Sultan Abdul Hamid: 'The way to get rid of the Armenian question is to get rid of the Armenians.' This is what had been carried out, with more thoroughness and bloodthirstiness than in the days of the sultan.

Some Armenians, he concluded, had been driven into the mountains, and were defending themselves as best they could. Five thousand or so (the inhabitants of Musa Dagh) had recently been taken off by a French cruiser off the coast of Syria. In Sasun they were still defending themselves

(this was said more in hope than in truth). The people were not yet
extinct. Bryce said he had no information of the fact of whether the
Germans had promoted or encouraged the massacres, and so could not
express an opinion on that issue. But he thought that the best hope for the
remaining Armenians was pressure from neutral nations upon the German
government, 'namely, to tell the Turks that they have gone too far'. Bryce's
calm and untheatrical speech was typical of the man.[4]

Six weeks later the fate of the Armenians was discussed in the House
of Commons. The Liberal MP for Durham North-West, Aneurin
Williams, spoke on the subject. He referred to the Lords debate, and
pointed out that after it

> ... the great majority of reading and thinking people realized that for the
> first time that the greatest massacres in history had been taking place
> during the last five months. In that discussion ... there were laid bare the
> facts of a horror such as the world has never seen. There have been great
> conquerors who have slaughtered many thousands and perhaps up to a
> million men, but those occurrences have been spread over a great number
> of years. The Turkish authorities within the little time of five months
> proceeded systematically to exterminate a whole race out of their domin-
> ions. They did so not in thousands or in tens of thousands, but in hundreds
> of thousands. One estimate says that 500,000 persons were killed within
> the five months, while according to another estimate the number was as
> many as 800,000 killed. There have been massacres of the Armenians
> before this last one. Ten years ago 30,000 were massacred, and ten years
> before that 100,000. But those massacres, which made the world shudder
> at the time, shrink into insignificance beside these massacres which we
> have unconsciously been living through in the last six or seven months.
>
> Since that debate took place, later details have come in from many
> sources, from German and Swiss missionaries, from escaped refugees, from
> Europeans in Asiatic Turkey, and from sources of all kinds, and all
> supporting one another in the most astonishing way, so that the facts all
> hang together and so that, while perhaps it is impossible to be certain of
> this or that detail, there is no doubt whatever of the broad lines of the
> occurrences. They are not general statements, but are statements from
> different quarters, describing what happened at particular places at
> particular times, with the names of the people who suffered and with the
> names of the people who inflicted those horrors.
>
> The broad facts are these, that in May or thereabouts orders were sent
> through the executive authority ... systematically to nearly all the centres in
> Turkey where there was any considerable Armenian population. I believe
> I am right in saying that these orders can be traced as having been sent to
> some fifty places, and a uniform procedure was adopted. The Armenians

of the particular centre concerned were collected together at short notice, sometimes within a few hours. In some instances where a time had been fixed the gendarmes arrived before the time, the Armenians were hustled out of their beds. Sometimes a little longer, up to ten or twelve days, but I believe never more than a fortnight was given. It was not men of military age that were taken to be interned. Not at all. The Armenians of military age were already serving Turkey as soldiers in the ranks, except those who were exempted under the laws of Turkey. At this time the men from fifteen to seventy who had not been taken as soldiers were collected together, and for the most part shot. The older men, the women and the children, were ordered to prepare to go away to a great distance. This did not take place simply in one town, but in practically every town where there was an Armenian population of any importance. It did not occur owing to the fanaticism of one particular magistrate or one particular population. It is what took place in obedience to the orders sent round from the central authorities.

These people were marched away, under the control of gendarmes to some extent, but to a large extent under the control of gaol birds – criminals who had been taken out of the gaols for the express purpose of being put in charge of these parties of Armenians. The people were allowed to take very little money with them, and very little food was given to them on the journey. In some cases they were allowed to hire carts, in which either to ride themselves or to take their belongings. In many cases these carts were turned back after a few hours or a few days of the journey had been accomplished, and the people were obliged to go on on foot. Sometimes, when they had gone a few days' journey, they were abandoned by their guards and told that they might go on by themselves. Then, when they had gone on a few miles, Kurds or other brigands fell upon them, robbed and murdered them, violated the women, took the children, and committed every kind of outrage and horror upon them ... Sò they went on, the people dropping by the way from hunger, women going absolutely naked in many cases, having been robbed of their clothes; babies were born by the roadside, and the mothers were told to go on and on, until they died ... finally, when they reached the River Euphrates, the women in many cases threw themselves into the river in order that they might escape by death from man's inhumanity.

Thus perhaps one third, or less than one third, of those who set out came to their destinations. What were those destinations? They were humorously called by the Turkish authorities agricultural colonies. They were, as a matter of fact, places in horrible swamps, or in some cases desert places where there was no water and no possibility of cultivation ... There they arrived in a perishing condition, and there those who are not yet dead are probably dying rapidly.[5]

Another speech outlining the grim fate of the Armenians followed, given by T. P. O'Connor, Liberal member for the Scotland division of Liverpool. Replying for the government, Foreign Office minister Lord Robert Cecil paid tribute to the two speakers, and said that he had little to add. He said that he would not harrow the feelings of the House by adding to the details of what occurred. 'It is enough to say that no element of horror, outrage, torture or slaughter was absent from this crime. It was not only the slaughter and destruction of this people, but it was the slaughter of them under the cruellest possible circumstances to be imagined.' Lord Robert pointed out that there was 'only one mitigation of the horror', and that was that the events 'had nothing to do with religious persecution or religious hatred'. It was by contrast a premeditated crime, a 'deliberate policy to destroy and wipe out of existence the Armenians in Turkey. It was systematically carried out. It was ordered from above, and when, as happened on one or two occasions, the local governors were anxious to spare some of the children, or mitigate in some degree the horrors of the operation, they were sternly ordered to go on with their work, and I believe in one or perhaps two cases they were removed from their offices for not carrying it out with sufficient vigour.'

Lord Robert then took issue with the idea that the Armenians had been in revolt, and even that British agents had encouraged the Armenians to rise in revolt, and that the events were thus merely 'a rough suppression of insurrection and riot'. These claims, he said, were without foundation, and Britain had certainly not intrigued with Armenians to stir up rebellion. 'The crime was a deliberate one, not to punish insurrection but to destroy the Armenian race. That was the sole object, the sole reason for it.'[6]

Lord Robert was pressed by supporters of the Armenians to offer practical support for them, which he could not do in view of the military situation. He was reminded of the rescue by the French, in September 1915, in a bold and daring escapade, of the villagers from Musa Dagh; might British naval vessels keep a look-out for similar events? His responses indicated scepticism. However the British government performed a great service for the Armenians in making public their sufferings, and not keeping them quiet for nebulous reasons of security. Today, one only has to read the evidence compiled in the British Blue Book, as well as the debates in the House, to see that those who now deny such events are concocters of fiction.

The Blue Book which was published by authority contained documents relating to the mass-extermination of Armenians. This volume, classed as Miscellaneous no 31 (1916), was also published commercially by Hodder and Stoughton with the title *The Treatment of Armenians in the Ottoman Empire*. Bryce supplied the preface, in which he scrupulously weighed up the validity of the evidence of the documents in the volume. He noted that much of the evidence came from eye-witnesses, and that 'when the same fact is stated by witnesses who had no communication with one another and in many cases did not even speak the same language, the presumption of its truth becomes strong.' To be absolutely sure he was not being misled, he gave copies of the evidence to three independent assessors: the historian Professor H. A. L. Fisher, vice-chancellor of Sheffield University, subsequently minister of education in Lloyd George's cabinet, and author of a three-volume *History of Europe*; the great classicist, Professor Gilbert Murray; and to the ex-President of the American Bar Association, Mr Moorfield Storey.

All three agreed that the documents bore the hallmark of truth. Fisher noted the 'countless scattered pieces of mutual corroboration'.[7] Murray pointed out that 'the statements of the Armenian refugees themselves are fully confirmed by residents of American, Scandinavian and even of German nationality; and the undesigned agreement between so many credible witnesses from widely separate districts puts all the main lines of the story beyond the possibility of doubt.'[8] Storey had no doubt that the statements established without any question the essential facts.[9]

Much of the editing of the documents was done anonymously by the young Arnold Toynbee, working from the Foreign Office. He wrote an editorial note at the beginning. In this he boldly stated that 'the editor is certain in his own mind that all the documents published here are genuine statements of truth, and he presents them in this assurance.' He assessed the different types of evidence contained, and noted that the total body of evidence was large – something that was remarkable in view of the stringent Ottoman censorship operating at the time and the atmosphere of totalitarian fear fostered by the Young Turk government.

At the end of the volume Toynbee wrote a 60-page essay on the history, geography and population distribution of the Armenians.[10] This is a fine summary, which repays study today. The passages on the ancient and medieval history of Armenia are of characteristic breadth and originality – although, as elsewhere in Toynbee's writing, on occasion one searches for incisiveness, pungency and irony, and an adherence to empirical fact.

Toynbee is perhaps at his best when refuting the pro-Turkish arguments about the destruction of the Ottoman Armenian community during the war. At the outset he points out the enormous losses suffered by the Armenians, and says categorically that 'no provocation or misdemeanour on the part of individual Armenians could justify such a crime against the whole race.'[11] Three main arguments are cited by supporters of the Ottoman Turkish position.[12] The first is that in April 1915 the Armenians revolted in Van, to coincide with Russian troop movements. Toynbee rebuts this, by pointing out that the deportations began before the events in Van, which anyway were not a revolt but a legitimate self-defence. 'The Turks fired the first shot at Van on 20 April 1915; the first Armenians were deported from Zeitun on 8 April, and there is a record of their arrival in Syria as early as the 19th.' Moreover, he says, the deportation from Zeitun must have been premeditated, since Turkish immigrants from Thrace (known as *muhajirs*) were ready and waiting to take over the property of the deportees once they had moved off.

The second point was that there was a general conspiracy of Armenians throughout the Ottoman empire, to coincide with an Allied attack on the empire. This too, said Toynbee, was baseless. Revolution was alleged to have been plotted in Cilicia, to coincide with an allied landing; but no allied landing was made. Anyway most Armenian able-bodied men were serving in the Ottoman army. The arms held by the Armenians were not supplies of bombs and so forth, destined for an uprising, but the 'moderate number of rifles and revolvers' that they had been permitted to bear since the Young Turkish revolution of 1908.

The third was that the Armenians had enlisted in volunteer regiments in the Russian Caucasus, the same point dealt with by Aneurin Williams in the House of Commons. Toynbee points out that most of these were Armenians already from Russia, since Armenia was a country divided between two empires. 'It is a misfortune for any nation to be divided between two allegiances, especially when the states to which they owe them elect to go to war; but it is at least an alleviation of the difficulty, and one that does honour to both parties concerned, when either fraction of the divided nationality finds itself in sympathy, even under the test of war, with the particular state to which its allegiance is legally due. The loyalty of the Russian Armenians to Russia cast no imputation upon the Ottoman Armenians, and was of no concern to the Turks.' Toynbee then reminds his readers of the fact that the Armenian Dashnak party, on the eve of war, resolved not to throw its lot in with either side in the war.

> The various Turkish contentions thus fail, from first to last, to meet the point. They all attempt to trace the atrocities of 1915 to events arising out of the war; but they not only cannot justify them on the ground, they do not even suggest any adequate motive for their perpetration. It is evident that the war was merely an opportunity and not a cause – in fact that the deportation scheme, and all that it involved, flowed inevitably from the general policy of the Young Turkish government.[13]

Toynbee then proceeds with an analysis of the political tenets of the Young Turkish government, tracing the change from the cynical vacuities of Sultan Abdul Hamid to the chauvinistic excesses of the Turkey's then rulers. A section follows on the procedure of the deportation of the Armenians, paying close regard to chronology, and refuting any charge of Armenian rebellion. He places in chronological order the disarming of the Armenian soldiers who had enlisted in the Ottoman army, the brutal arms searches of March 1915, the assault on the Armenians of Van by the city's own governor, and then the indescribably horrific nature of the deportations themselves. He finds a clear pattern to the extermination, covering the months of April to September 1915. After assessing the numbers of the deportees, he places responsibility for the affairs entirely on the heads of the government.

The extraordinary thing about Toynbee is that, having argued so cogently and lucidly that the Young Turks were committing an appalling crime by their mass-slaughter of Armenians, later, arguing in a sophistical and fallacious manner, and manifesting an inability to distinguish between valid and invalid argumentation, he overturned his own arguments. Even though his careful chronology in the Blue Book proved that the Armenians had acted in self-defence, and not as fifth-columnists, he later repudiated that viewpoint, without adducing any new facts or employing any additional logical arguments for his new conclusion. His historiography retreated from the world of logical discourse into some strange world where greatness and narcissism coexist, where factual evidence and chronology were to be accounted lesser than the subjective impressions of a great man. His humility before dates and facts and places disappeared as he built up his own metaphysical system for history. In this way, the issues of the Armenian genocide disappeared from his horizons. It was almost as if the Armenians and the terrible events which had befallen them were not grand enough for Toynbee's new and sweeping vision of world history – a vision which was unquestionably exciting, but which was largely unanchored to the earlier discipline of attention to historical details.

The kindest interpretation that one can find is that Toynbee, tiring of exploring the light, clear side of the historical truth of the Near East, made a deliberate enquiry into the dark, shadow side of events there, something that responded to a need within his own psyche, and that in this process factual details and clear argument were dispensed with. Perhaps here was something open to interpretation from the standpoint of Jungian analytical psychology: Toynbee exploring the shadow-side of his own personality. But the process produced not truth but grandiosity: a personal view of power, in which the Armenians were too minor for consideration. The issues of the mass-extermination of the Armenians in 1915, and of their eviction from their ancient land, became lost. Lost, too, was informed and sympathetic support for the Armenians, at a time when their own losses were incalculable.

## CHAPTER 16

# 'A Stable and Civilizing Force'
## W. E. D. Allen

Immediately following the armistice of 1918, the representatives of the victorious Allies were convinced that Armenia had to be part of the settlement. The plight of the people roused sympathy world-wide, not just in Europe and America. But Armenia's wartime sufferings did not remain in the official memory for long. It became clear that the memory span of international statesmen of that time was short. By 1919, no public document was referring to the organized mass-killings of the Armenians, which had been officially detailed only three years earlier. The Armenians for their part appeared not to have kept specific details of the genocide in the public eye, but to have preferred to speak in general terms. There was little attempt to explore individual incidents or to look at the ideology that motivated their people's killers. As a result the issue was forgotten. The quarrels between Britain and France about mandates and spheres of influence became paramount; vendettas among the victors destroyed all chance of recompense for the Armenians. So too did the uncertainty of British policy in Transcaucasia, which was torn between the conflicting options of supporting the independent republics of Georgia, Armenia and Azerbaijan, and of backing the Volunteer Army of General Denikin, which sought to crush the republics and re-establish the tsarist autocracy.

Only scholars who anchored their work to facts, and charity workers, by this time remembered Armenians. Politicians were shown mostly to have used the Armenian issue to project images of themselves as caring; they were prepared to drop Armenia when they discovered the greater political excitement of quarrelling with former allies over markets, territory and access to raw materials. Lloyd George had made grandiloquent speeches in favour of the Armenians, when the issue was one that stirred his listeners, yet he created obstacles to their achieving anything in the settlement. Even in cabinet, in September 1918, he had backed the Turkish capture of Baku for the old regional reasons of Russophobia.

One soldier–scholar–politician who did write honestly on the

Armenians' behalf, though not all the time, was the Ulsterman W. E. D. ('Bill') Allen. He was a curious, highly interesting figure, whose true political identity and motives no one has yet cracked. Above all a scholar (though sometimes a wayward one), he was keen to keep the objective facts in mind; as a result, the condition and the reality of Armenia never disappeared from him as it did from other public figures who were less concerned with factual matters. He was briefly in Parliament as the Unionist MP for Belfast West in 1929–31. He was the author of *The Turks in Europe* (1922), and, following a visit to Soviet Georgia in 1926, a number of works on the history of that country. He became a member of Mosley's fascists in 1931 – almost certainly not out of conviction, but rather at the request of the security services, for whom he was probably working. Under the pseudonym of James Drennan he wrote a favourable study of the fascist movement entitled *B.U.F.: Oswald Mosley and British Fascism*. With the onset of war he abandoned dabbling in fascism, either as observer or participant, and, as a captain in the Life Guards, served in Ethiopia and the Middle East.

In 1944–46 Bill Allen published his first full length work of military history, in collaboration with Professor Paul Muratoff of Moscow, a former artillery officer in the imperial armies, who had left the Soviet state in 1922. The subject was the Russian campaigns of 1941–45 (two volumes, Penguin). The two authors later collaborated on a masterpiece of military history, *Caucasian Battlefields* (Cambridge, 1953; long out of print). Allen served as press attaché in the British Embassy in Ankara from 1945 to 1949, at the inception of the Cold War. This was a very sensitive position. He paid another visit to Soviet Georgia at around the same time. In 1948 the presence in the British Embassy in Ankara of a former alleged fascist supporter was the subject of some angry questions in the House of Commons. Later he retired to Whitechurch House, Co. Waterford, where he and his fourth wife dispensed hospitality to scholars and historians from across the globe. He died in 1973. His library is now housed at the University of Michigan.

In the January 1920 issue of the *Quarterly Review*, Bill Allen wrote an article entitled 'The Armenians: their past and their future'. It has to be said that this article contains a number of somewhat crude clubland generalizations about the nation. Allen was in that respect being true to his class, or rather to his adopted class – for however much he might write derogatively about the Armenians for their smartness at 'trade', no one could disguise the fact that the Belfast advertising firm of David Allen and Co. was one of the most successful businesses in the province. Bill Allen however redeemed any prejudices by his scholarship and his perceptiveness.[1]

Two qualities stood out in his writing about the Caucasus. One was his feeling for the geography of the region. In this he resembled Lynch. He understood the military consequences of the disposition of Armenia's mountains. Secondly, and relatedly, he understood the scope and limits of imperial power. He did not waste time in expatiating on religious differences. He got down to the essentials of power, and analysed them clearly. These aspects of his writing made up for the occasional unscholarly generalization, or error of fact, and, typically for the British at that time, for ignoring large areas of the culture of the Caucasian peoples, notably, in the case of the Armenians, the achievement of early medieval architecture and manuscript illumination. His essay is remarkable achievement for a 19 year old, showing unusual historical breadth.

> Combining the artistic intelligence of the Persian with the commercial acumen of the Greek and the steady industry of the German, the Armenians should have held a prominent place among the nations by whom European civilization was developed. But from her geographical position between the eastern and western seats of civilization and the northern and southern breeding-grounds of the young and savage races who from century to century assailed these civilizations, Armenia became from earliest times the battle-ground of contending nations, and the Armenians were the victims of all the great historical changes which disturbed the neighbouring lands. Only in the brief intervals, when the power of the contiguous imperial peoples was declining, were the Armenians able to assert their independence and to develop their national individuality ...
>
> Eventually towards the end of the ninth century, the decline of the Caliphate occasioned an Armenian revival; the Bagratuni family at Ani and the Ardzruni at Van established little feudal monarchies. For a brief moment in his weary chronicle of wars and the rumours thereof, the venerable chronicler John Catholicos gives us the picture of a happy community of farmers and husbandmen enjoying the riches which nature has given to them.
>
> Lands were bestowed [he says]; vines were planted and groves of olive-trees; the most ancient of fruit trees yielded their fruit. The harvest produced corn in excessive abundance; the cellars were filled with wine when the vintage had been gathered in. The mountains were in great joy and so were the herdsmen and the shepherds, because of the quantity of the pasturage and the increase in the flock.
>
> But neither the Bagratuni nor the Ardzruni succeeded in building up an organized national state. Perhaps the Armenian renaissance had come too early; the feudal organization of the country made it impossible to unite against the invaders.
>
> At the beginning of the eleventh century, a fresh wave of barbarian invasion began to sweep across the Middle East ... But foreign conquest and

alien rule in its most brutal form alike failed to eliminate the Armenians as a race. Throughout the long centuries of Turkish domination they maintained their independence and individuality in thought and religion. A national church, antiquated though it might be in dogma and practice, and a national literature, beautiful in expression and profound in sentiment, kept alive the memory of a legendary liberty which had never been very real ...

The treaties of Turkmanchai (1828) and Adrianople definitely established the Russians in Transcaucasia; and with this event opened the modern phase of the Armenian question.

The condition of the Armenians was indubitably ameliorated. Under the Russian government they were accorded some degree of autonomy in educational and ecclesiastical affairs, and an administration which brought peace, if not liberty and justice. For 80 years the Armenians of Transcaucasia showed little discontent with Russian rule ... Against the Turkish Armenians the full vigour of Mahmud II's Europeanized bureaucracy was directed. While Stratford de Redcliffe was at Constantinople, some attempt was made to obtain recognition of their primary rights by the institution of an Armenian National Council; and in the treaties of Paris and Berlin certain provisions were inserted in their favour. But Abdul Hamid was astute enough to see that the differences among the powers on the subject of the eastern question would prevent them from combining to enforce these provisions, and with calculated brutality he set himself to carry out his policy of Turkification by the deliberate extermination of the Armenians. In the restless Kurdish hill-men, ever jealous of the industrious Armenian cultivator, he found willing tools, who proceeded to carry out that ghastly series of massacres from the year 1894 onwards. 'There is no exaggeration', wrote Sir W. M. Ramsay, 'in the worst accounts of the horrors of Armenia ... Armenia is "the black country" ... It has become a charnel house.'[2]

In 1908, when the Young Turks overthrew the incompetent autocracy of Yildiz and announced the millennium, the Turkish Armenians accepted with enthusiasm the doctrine of an 'Ottoman People, One and Indivisible'; and for a few months it seemed as though the Armenian might fraternize with the Turk in the heaven of Ahmed Riza. But the Adana massacres proved that a vigorous oligarchy had but succeeded a decaying despotism. The Young Turks proceeded to 'Turkify' all their subject peoples, even Arabs – and Albanians, the favoured of Abdul Hamid; and the Armenians were submitted to the same process ...

There is not space here to recount the part played by the Armenians in the Caucasus campaigns ... in the terrible and critical winter of 1917–18, when the Treaty of Brest–Litovsk was being negotiated, and the Russian soldiery was swarming into Tiflis and up the Dariel Pass, Armenian troops, in spite of disaster and treachery in the rear, continued to resist the Turkish advance into Transcaucasia.

It cannot be denied that the Allied powers have treated a people who have sacrificed a third of their population in support of the Allied cause, with a callousness which would be deserving of condemnation in the case of a defeated enemy. In November 1918 the Erivan government requested official recognition, financial assistance for reconstruction, and the reunion of all Armenian troops serving in the Allied armies, 'to serve as a nucleus, with the assistance of Allied officers, of a new Armenian army.' These demands were ignored at Paris. A 'reunion' of troops, similar to that suggested by the Erivan government, was facilitated in the cases of Poland, Yugoslavia and Czechoslovakia. General Torcom, the chief of the Armenian Military Mission in London, drew up detailed plans for the organization and employment of repatriated Armenian troops. Their arrival in Transcaucasia would have permitted the earlier withdrawal of the British army of occupation, and would have given the Erivan government the strength and the opportunity to establish themselves in towns so definitely Armenian as Kars, Erzerum and Van. But the British authorities neglected General Torcom's proposals.

Allen here sets out proposals for borders and mandates of a future Armenia and Kurdistan, parts of which rather rapidly dated; however the following remained significant.

The vilayets [provinces] of Trebizond, Erzerum and Van would remain to constitute the western portion of independent Armenia, and would afford an ample area of settlement for the hundreds of thousands of refugees in the governments [provinces] of Erivan and Kars. It might be added that it would be necessary to guarantee a local autonomy to the Greeks of the Pontine littoral – a condition which carries the approval of M. Venizelos. To the three vilayets should be added those districts of the governments of Erivan and Kars in which the Armenians are numerically predominant. Such an addition involves the larger question of the eventual independence or autonomy of the border races of the former Russian empire. Whatever be the future form of government in Russia, this is a question which should not be allowed to remain in doubt. Self-determination for the border-races must be the basis of any agreement with established authority in Russia. At the same time Russia must not be given to think that Britain desires to impose her hegemony in Transcaucasia. Whatever assistance, British or American, is given to the Transcaucasian republics, it should be made clear that it is intended that these countries shall eventually be either independent or members of a Russian Federated Republic.

Black as is the present prospect, there is no reason why Armenia should not prosper as a nation. There are in Armenia all the elements that should go to form a people capable of self-government – an heroic soldiery, an industrious peasantry, an intelligent bourgeoisie. The New Armenia should have a population of from two to three millions, and the country could support four times that number; the Armenians are a prolific people, and, free from the perils of massacre, expropriation and famine, they should multiply quickly. Established in their independence and secure in their liberty, the Armenians will form a stable and civilizing force for the regeneration of the Nearer East. In bloodshed and sorrow they have earned their right to freedom – their right to work and live.[3]

Thirty-three years later Bill Allen published, with Paul Pavlovich Muratoff (who had died before the work's publication) *Caucasian Battlefields*. This book is still much sought after, as an indispensable guide to the military situation along the Caucasian frontier. Curiously, in view of its objectivity and importance, it has not been subjected to a critique either by Ottoman specialists or Turkish lobbyists. Maybe this is because it presents no evidence for a 'civil war' between Armenians and Turks at the time of the first world war.

Here the authors discuss the state of affairs in the Caucasus following the collapse of the Russian front after the Bolshevik Revolution of November 1917.

By 1 January 1918 the Armenian Corps consisted of two divisions of Armenian rifles, three brigades of Armenian volunteers, a cavalry brigade and some battalions of militia. Each of the two divisions was composed of four regiments, regimental strength being fixed at three battalions. The volunteer brigades were made up of four battalions each and the cavalry brigade was composed of two regiments each four squadrons strong. The rifle divisions were made up of men from the Armenian rifle *druzhiny* (battalions) which had seen hard and honourable fighting during the campaigns of 1914–16. Their numbers were increased by Armenians from different units of Yudenich's army who had decided to join their compatriots. The volunteers were natives of Turkish Armenia who joined the national army on the spot – in Erzincan, Erzurum, Van and the Eleşkirt valley. There was no lack of good equipment to be acquired in the rear areas of Yudenich's dissolving army, and the infantry was well provided with machine guns. The artillery might have been stronger but for the lack of trained gunners available among the Armenians. However, six batteries (each of four field guns) represented the artillery of each of the two divisions, while mountain batteries were organized for attachment to the three volunteer brigades. Units were weak in effectives: the strength of a battalion fluctuated between 400 and 600 men. Thus with twenty-four battalions of riflemen and eight battalions of volunteers, the Armenian national army did not exceed 16,000 infantry, 1000 cavalry and some 4000 militiamen. Even with the help of 10,000 Georgians (whose morale was doubtful) such a small army could not hope to hold a Turkish offensive, particularly when it is remembered that the luckless Armenians were dependent on long and disorganized lines of communication ...

It would have been strange if the Young Turk government of Enver Paşa had not considered the revolution in Russia as the predestined moment for the realization of all their ambitious schemes in the direction of the Caucasus. Pan-Turanian expansion might yet compensate for the loss, or impending loss, of the Arab provinces. Even the less romantic circles in the army might at least find the moment opportune for the recovery of the traditional frontier of 1878. During the middle months of 1917 the Turks were attentively observing the course of events in Russia. By the end of the year it was decided that the moment had come to pass to action. For this action the Third Army under Vehip Paşa had been reserved; and it explains why the Turks, despite the complete lull on the Russian front and the urgent need for reinforcement on the fronts threatened by the British, kept the Third Army ear-marked for a Caucasian adventure.[4]

In early 1918 the Turks re-captured a few frontier posts from the Transcaucasian forces. Neither side considered that it was at war:

> The Turks might claim that they were re-occupying their own provinces. The Armenians, however, were confronted with a very special problem: the protection of the Armenian population in the districts which the Turks were in process of reoccupying. The issue of the peace negotiations [at Trebizond] was unknown, but immediate danger threatened all Armenians living in the regions of Erzurum, Hinis, Van, Malazgirt and the Eleşkirt plain. These unfortunate people preferred not to await the coming of the Turkish army and asked for immediate evacuation beyond the Transcaucasian border. To protect them and to give them time to withdraw, a considerable part of the new Armenian national army was dispersed between the various centres populated by Armenians. Erzurum was garrisoned by a detachment under command of the famous partisan leader Andranik (who had been promoted to the grade of major-general). Other detachments held Hinis and Van, while inside the old frontier two groups were concentrated at Aleksandropol and Erevan. This disposition was determined not by any strategic plan but by the protective necessities of the moment. Fears of the Tartars of Azerbaijan and Nahçivan imposed the relatively large reserve held behind the Aras.
>
> The small Armenian army was thus spread over a very wide area. In command was General Nazarbekov (Nazarbekian), an Armenian by origin, formerly commanding the 2nd Caucasian Rifle Division – an officer who had never been very fortunate in the field. A considerable number of imperial officers, the majority of them Armenians by origin but including also a number of Russians, made up the staff and the unit commands. About 300 young Russian officers had formed an officers' battalion which fought beside the Armenians.[5]

Despite small successes, the story of the early months of 1918 was of unrelenting Ottoman advances. The Turks first re-captured all of the Ottoman territory, then seized Kars, and finally pressed onwards through Transcaucasia to Baku. The authors comment that 'with only indefinite hopes of ultimate support from the British, the Armenians had no alternative but to show fight to the invader.'[6] By May 1918 'it has rarely fallen to the lot of a people to confront such a desperate and seemingly hopeless situation as that which threatened the Armenians in the early summer of 1918'.[7] The authors make a distinction between guerrilla war and partisan war (Allen's own experiences in Ethiopia obviously had relevance here), and comment that Armenian terrain favoured partisan strategy, whose characteristic was compact mobile detachments, each 500–1500 strong, equipped with field guns and machine guns. 'For such a war the Armenians had excellent leaders – famous partisan chiefs like Antranik, Amazasp and Dro.' However, the military leaders of the new Armenian government, trained in the old school, persisted in believing they were commanding a 'regular' national army in a regular war.

Things looked bad around Karakilisa, east of Aleksandropol, in May of 1918. Nazarbekov and Andranik both recorded losses. But around Erevan, General Silikov (or Silikian) took on the Turkish army at Sardarabad, west of Echmiadzin; and Dro was dispatched north of Erevan with 1000 riflemen to guard the defile of Baş Abaran. Allen and Muratoff continue:

> On 20 May units of the Turkish 12th Infantry Division occupied Igdir. The Armenians concentrated the 1st and 2nd Van Regiments and the cavalry regiment on the northern bank of the Aras defending the bridges at Markara and Karakale. On the 21st, Silikov's main group was attacked near Sardarabad by two regiments of the Turkish 11th Caucasian Division on the march from Aleksandropol. The Armenians were holding the line of villages, Kurakanlu–Kerpalu–Zeiva, a few miles to the west of their holy city and patriarchal seat of Echmiadzin. The Turks were not in greater force than the Armenians and, using all his reserve, Silikov successfully counter-attacked on 23 and 24 May. He not only recaptured Sardarabad but pressed back the enemy as far as Ani and Mastara, some thirty miles to the north of Sardarabad. The same day Dro was fighting the 3rd Regiment of the 11th Caucasian Division, which was advancing from Amamli to Bas–Abaran. Silikov reinforced him with the 2nd Cavalry Regiment and on the 25th Dro counter-attacked. Fighting continued on the 26th, and on the 28th Dro was reinforced by infantry sent up by Silikov. On the 29th he was able to throw back the Turks to the north of Baş Abaran, and remained in firm possession of this important defile.

Thus both Silikov and Dro, operating on terms of numerical equality with the enemy, had each secured an important success.[8]

Indeed they had. The victory of Sardarabad assured the existence of the Republic of Armenia, and perhaps the very continuation of the Armenian nation. Silikov and Dro showed astonishing bravery and competence in these engagements – and it was their good fortune to have had their achievements described by a brilliant Ulsterman, who was both scholar and soldier.

## CHAPTER 17

# 'To Regain Their Self-Respect by Useful Labour'
## Dr Armstrong Smith, Revd Harold Buxton
## and Dudley Northcote

In 1916 a delegation from the London-based Armenian (Lord Mayor's) Fund travelled to the Russian Caucasus, to assess the scale of the disaster that had befallen the Armenians across the border in Ottoman lands, and to give assistance to the survivors who had escaped into Transcaucasia. This visit marked the beginning of about a decade of British assistance in the region for those dislocated in the course of war, revolution, invasion and massacre. Most of the help went to Armenians, because they had been targeted for destruction and hence the needs of their survivors were greatest. With the collapse of the tsarist armies in 1917 contact with the region was broken, but charity resumed after the armistice of the following year. Throughout the years of the first independent Republic of Armenia, British aid-workers worked in Transcaucasia; and after the proclamation of Armenia as a Soviet state in December 1920, they stayed on. Communism and capitalism coexisted, without the paranoia which usually characterized the proximity of the two systems.

In 1922 Dr Armstrong Smith, of the Save the Children Fund, travelled to the region, and his report was published as a pamphlet entitled *Famine in Transcaucasia*, with an introduction by the philanthropist and humanitarian the Revd Harold Buxton, who had visited Transcaucasia with his brother Noel in 1913. Buxton highlighted the dislocation that the war had brought to Transcaucasia, formerly a rich region. He noted the slow speed of change in the countryside. 'One has only to travel a mile or two from the railway in any part of the Caucasus to find a village life as simple and primitive as that which prevails in Turkey or Persia.' Buxton was also a realist. As an aid-worker, he had no time for myths.

> The peasantry, whether mountaineers or plainsmen, and no matter of what nationality, are far from having the ferocious character which romantic writers have attributed to them. By nature they are, generally speaking, quiet, diligent and law-abiding folk, content with a minimum of comfort,

requiring very little of imported goods and tolerant of any form of government which leaves them alone and does not impose excessive burdens upon them. But these last years of turmoil in Transcaucasia have thrown the rural population into worse and worse confusion resulting in an almost total neglect or abandonment of certain districts, and at the same time in a most serious reduction in the food production of the country. The destruction of human life, and the shifting of whole groups of villagers from one district to another, have been accompanied by the loss of agricultural equipment and of draught animals, and by the falling into utter disrepair of roads, bridges, irrigation canals, etc.[1]

Dr Armstrong Smith's report is of great interest. He arrived in Yerevan on 20 April 1922, and soon afterwards visited the British feeding station there, which looked after 450 children.

The station is placed, owing to the extreme lack of accommodation in Erivan, in a large disused wine cellar. The majority of the children are from poor families of the town, children either who have only a mother or whose father has no employment. These families are nearly all from Turkish Armenia and Kars, and there is little prospect of their becoming self-supporting till they can return to their homes. The present condition of most of these children is very different from what it was only three months ago, when the feeding was started. There were also a number of children who have no homes, and are at present housed in a shelter house until there is a possibility of their being taken into an orphanage. There are constant applications to the office on behalf of other children, and when means allow, Mr Harcourt [the Rev. H. W. Harcourt, chief British aid worker in Armenia] is anxious at least to double the number fed in Erivan alone. This will now be possible with the arrival of the SCF supplies. The Americans are already feeding about 1600 children in the town. Day by day children are drifting in from the villages owing to the scarcity of food and to the death of their parents by starvation. The American and British Committees have cleared the streets of Erivan of homeless children at least twice this winter, but their number is again increasing.

We then walked on through the town to one of the market gardens, which were derelict, and have been cleaned up and planted by refugee labour. The men are rationed with supplies sent by Miss Emily Robinson's Committee [the Armenian Red Cross and Refugee Fund] and paid a small sum, 20,000,000 roubles a day (2s 6d [12½p]) ... The area which has up to the present been cleared is about 25 acres. A fresh gang of men start next Monday clearing up one of the ruined quarters of the town which is to be turned into public gardens. This work has been initiated and organized by Mr [Dudley] Northcote, formerly of the civil administration of Mesopotamia ... I was very glad to observe that the adult relief was being given in return for work and the labour of the refugees turned towards the reconstruction of the town. In other words, the policy of the Lord Mayor's Fund is to help these necessitous people to regain their self-respect by useful labour.

Our next visit was to the British Orphanage (Lord Mayor's Fund). During our walk through the town one was struck by its terribly delapidated condition – whole quarters are in ruins, and the appearance of the place plainly shows the result of the last four years' incessant conflict and chaos. The orphanage was established in 1918 at Igdir, one of the towns seized by the Turks during their raid on Armenia in 1920. The initiation of the orphanage is due to Mr Sarkis Topalian, who is now a student of the London School of Oriental Studies, and the *esprit de corps* is largely due to his influence. When Igdir was threatened by the Kurds the children were transferred first to Nork and finally to the building they now occupy at Erivan. There are 150 children, boys and girls, 30 of whom have been taken off the streets during the last six months.

The manageress is an Armenian lady of Van, Miss Satenik Babikian, who puts her whole heart and soul into the work. I was much impressed with the cleanliness and good order of the institution, in view of the very great difficulty in housing so many children in a building of its size. Mr Harcourt told me that when the number reached 90 he decided that no more could be taken. However, necessity knows no law. The children were neatly dressed, and quite evidently well fed and very happy. The absence of the usual institutional tone and the family atmosphere that was apparent pleased me much. It is an advantage for Armenia to have such an institution in its midst to create a standard for the government orphanages, and Mr Harcourt is much to be congratulated on this piece of work. I had the pleasure a few days later of spending an afternoon with these children, and was much impressed with the kindliness and good feeling that prevailed in this large family. I have visited orphanages in many countries and nowhere is there a greater endeavour to make up to the children for want of family life ...[2]

On Monday, the 24th, we motored out to Kamarlu [modern Artashat], situated 28 versts [18 miles] from Erivan. On the way we passed through one of the richer districts of the republic, and it was very satisfactory to see how much land was sown and how promising the crops looked. I was told that this was due in large measure to the efforts of Mr [Aramayis] Yerzinkian, the Commissar of Agriculture. We passed through a succession of villages, each one of which showed the terrible effects of the Turkish invasion and the civil war. Very many houses and even complete villages were in utter ruin, and much land and many vineyards had gone out of cultivation ...

On arrival at Kamarlu we visited the British feeding station, at which 400 children are given a daily meal. Some of these children come from great distances. Mr Grant, who is in charge of the British relief work in this district, told me of cases in which children came from a distance of 10 versts (6½ miles) in order to be fed ... We were invited to visit one of the government orphanages. The children appeared to have enough to eat, but their quarters and their beds showed the extremely meagre resources of the government. I was glad to see, however, that the children had at least good underclothing, which I found was furnished from the Manchester committee material. The garments had been made up at the British committee workrooms by women employed by means of Miss Robinson's fund. If those kind friends could see the children whom their gifts have benefited they would feel amply repaid for their efforts to relieve the misery in this desolated region, and I pray them not to relax their efforts, for the needs will be great for some time yet ...

Before the war Kamarlu was a prosperous little town of some 5,000 inhabitants, containing many cognac factories and surrounded by areas of cotton plantations and vineyards. Today more than half of the town is in ruins. The cognac factories have ceased work, and cotton is cultivated scarcely at all. In these times of famine the peasants naturally prefer to grow foodstuffs, but the government is making great efforts this year to re-introduce the cotton cultivation, and to this end have imported a large quantity of cotton seed from Turkestan. This is being issued to the peasants who receive a bread allowance, and are to return a portion of the crop to the government ...[3]

### Etchmiadzin

On Tuesday, April 25th, the government was good enough to place at our disposal a motor car and one of their officers to escort us to the district of Etchmiadzin. The distance to this town was 12 miles, and we were glad to observe that, where possible, both sides of the road were ploughed up and planted. At the town of Etchmiadzin we visited the refugees' headquarters. In the town itself there are about 10,000 inhabitants, of which 1,500 are refugees and are said to be on the verge of starvation. Mr [Arshak] Safrastian [from London: the interpreter] and I personally inspected some 800 of these poor people, who have fled, most of them, from the Kars and Igdir areas. In the poor quarters in which some of them are housed we did not see a particle of bread or other food, but on close examination we found them cooking roots, herbs and grass. It is not surprising, therefore, that dysentery is very prevalent. We saw many cases of starving adults, many of whom will certainly die in a few days unless help is forthcoming. The Revkom [revolutionary committee] is drawing up a statement which it will submit to Mr Harcourt, who has promised to consider opening a feeding station as soon as possible after the SCF food arrives, and after consultation with the NER [Near East Relief], which has just begun work in this district. . .

The next day ... we again motored to Etchmiadzin, and were asked by the chairman of the Revkom to visit the villages near the Turkish frontier along the banks of the Arax river. We passed five or six villages which were totally destroyed during the Turkish invasion of 1920, and, with the exception of one village, there did not appear to be a soul in these places; the devastation was complete. We were told that these villages were typical of some 20 others of the district, which had been destroyed at the same time. We motored to the frontier village of Markara on the left bank of the river Arax, across which was a bridge, with Russian sentries on one side and Turkish on the other. Markara was crowded with Armenians of the district because there was a small garrison there, and consequently the village had been rebuilt to some extent. The misery and destitution throughout this district was greater than anything I had previously seen. On the return journey we met an old woman and her daughter, who showed us the bread she had made, a specimen of which I am bringing to England. It consisted chiefly of clay, dust and flour-mill sweepings, black and gritty and almost devoid of nourishment.

I had the honour of being received by His Holiness the Catholicos at the monastery of Etchmiadzin. He is a very venerable old gentleman, who inquired anxiously whether Britain intended abandoning Armenia altogether. He emphasized the great sacrifices which this Christian people had suffered in the cause of the Allies during the war. One of his bishops showed us over the museum, in which were priceless treasures, such as paintings, coins, tapestries, manuscripts and other antiquities of great historic interest. Etchmiadzin is a monastery which has been, from the time Armenia became Christian, the centre of her people's religious life and a great seat of learning ... With the destruction of the country in the last few years, Etchmiadzin has suffered too, bit there is no doubt – since it holds such a place in the hearts of Armenians all over the world – that with the reconstruction of the country which will come with security, it will soon regain its former glory. On all sides I hear great appreciation of Mr Buxton's efforts on behalf of justice and security for the Armenian people.

Our relations with the Revkom were most cordial, and the members expressed great appreciation of my visit. I was able to tell them that Mr Harcourt would consider most sympathetically the possibility of opening a feeding station for children immediately the food arrived.[4]

## Erivan

We returned to Erivan just in time to attend a performance at the local theatre by the children of the British orphanage. The programme consisted of dances, songs, recitations and a short play, all of which were of exceptional interest and artistically carried out. Very great credit is due to Miss Satenik Babikian. It was difficult to believe that many of these children were picked up in the streets only a few months ago in a dirty, starving and quite vagabond condition. Unfortunately, many such children are still to be seen in the countryside.

I met one little boy with a very interesting history, which is no doubt typical of a large number of children in the orphanages. He is little more than ten years old, yet his wanderings over the Caucasus would compare favourably with many a Fellow of the Royal Geographical Society. So far as can be gathered, he, with his father, fled from one of the villages near Erzerum during the massacres of the war period. With the retreating Russian army they went to the neighbourhood of Novo Rossisk in the North Caucasus, returning at a later date to Kars. Here they were caught by the Turkish invasion of 1920. The father was taken by the Turks and the boy never heard of him again. He himself wandered out of the Turkish lines and moved about seeking food from town to town during the winter of 1920 and the early part of 1921. In this period he visited Tiflis, Karakilisa, Delijan and Alexandropol [today Tbilisi, Vanadzor, Dilijan and Gyumri]. When picked up he was found travelling on an engine from Karakilisa to Alexandropol in utter rags with billy-can and little satchel. He speaks Armenian, Turkish and Russian. In spite of this period of vagabondage he is now quite unspoilt and not the least self-conscious, has charming manners and readily responds to what is being done for him.

In many other countries, children can be saved without the need of establishing special institutions. Unfortunately, in Armenia there are tens of thousands of children who have lost both parents, and whose other relations, if they exist, are in the condition of refugees. At the same time, owing to the small resources of the present Armenia and the widespread destruction of nearly every district, the government can do little to help them ... Surely nowhere in the world are there so many children whose pitiable condition appeals to humanity for assistance ...[5]

The following will give an example of the economic state of the country. Until recently 50,000 rouble notes were the highest denomination in circulation. The value of the Armenian rouble has degenerated to such an extent that 175,000,000 can now be purchased for one pound sterling; in other words, 3,500 of these 50,000 notes. One pound's worth of these notes actually weighs 8 lbs. This necessitates the employment of an ox-cart to carry the monthly salaries to the LMF [Lord Mayor's Fund] employees. A certain fisherman from Lake Sevan came to Erivan with 10 poods (360 lbs) of fish. He sold his fish, and returned to his village with exactly the same weight in paper money which he had received in payment! The price of good writing paper is such that the 50,000 rouble note covers a greater area of paper than can be bought for its face value. As it no longer therefore pays to print 50,000 rouble notes, the government has been compelled to issue a higher denomination, and a few days ago a 25,000,000 note appeared. This is at present the highest denomination, and equals less than three shillings [15p]. A pound (14 ozs) of bread costs 2,500,000 roubles, and a box of matches half a million. Foreign trade is only able to exist because of the cheques of the relief societies sold in Erivan. The country is overcrowded with Turkish-Armenian refugees (Erivan for example had before the war a population of not more than 30,000 people; now, with one third of its houses destroyed, it contains about 100,000), and has a far larger population than it can support at its present development. Before the war Armenia exported cotton, wine, brandy and canned fruit to Russia, and received in return wheat and flour. War has destroyed trade, and the peasants have had to grow food for themselves.

In spite of great difficulties ... the LMF is doing splendid work in Armenia which will materially and morally help towards the reconstruction of the country. Mr Harcourt and his colleagues are to be congratulated on the success they have already achieved and the promise of the future, especially in view of the small number of persons engaged in supervising and planning this big work. It has been my privilege to see much relief work in many countries, and nowhere have I seen a mission working under greater difficulties and with such determination, perseverance and enthusiasm.[6]

## THE REVD HAROLD BUXTON

Harold Buxton was one of the most clear-headed and steadfast friends of the Armenians. No personal vanity, or systems of power or paranoia, deflected his vision from a concern for what he actually saw; which was, the destitution of the Armenian villagers first under the rule of Ottoman Turkey, and then as refugees from Turkey in Russian Armenia. Those were the axiomatic considerations in his assessment of the situation in the Caucasus; and any consideration which failed to give primacy to this human situation was of little value, according to him. His preface to Dr Armstrong Smith's SCF report indicates his persistent effort to de-mythologize the region.

Buxton had been in Armenia with his brother Noel before the outbreak of the war. He revisited Yerevan in 1916 to assess the needs of the refugees; he also travelled to the front with the Russian armies, 'beyond Erzerum, and later at Van'. His third visit to Armenia was after the country had become Soviet, in the winter of 1921-22. Drawing on these experiences, he wrote a short book for the Faith Press entitled *Trans-Caucasia* (1926) containing details and reflections on the three major nationalities of the region, and on the situation in the Caucasus in general. Buxton shows few traces of partisanship, despite his primary sympathy for Armenia.

One recalls many scenes as the following. Midnight; a Caucasian railway station. We had been forty hours on the train, herded in dark compartments, with no glass (boards only) in the window frames. Our food supplies had run out in the first twenty-four hours, and we were hungry, sleepless and dirty beyond description. One felt a ruthless impatience with all the world, and particularly with those human beings who, carrying loads of unpleasant parasites, kept pressing their unpleasant bodies upon one. Dumped out in pitch darkness, we found ourselves in a worse 'jam' than ever. We had to choose between the crowd on the platform plus a freezing wind, and the crowd in the waiting room, plus a foul and foetid atmosphere. We went in. We sat down on our baggage, wedged firmly in the crowd, unable to distinguish the faces of those nearest us. All at once daylight came; and the violent repulsion one felt towards this stinking mass of humanity began to dissolve when one saw how far worse off these people were than ourselves. I was accustomed to hearing Georgian, Turkish, Armenian. These were Russian words, piteously sobbed out by a child. Then someone cursed: 'More Volga children ... came in an hour ago.' Mentally one registered another curse upon those responsible for these circumstances. Without parents, friends, food or shelter, these little starved, naked scraps of humanity flying from famine on the Volga had come to find certain death here.

Many among us have been accustomed to associate the Armenian question exclusively with Turkey. It is important that they should now realize that the future of the Armenians is bound up with that of Russia. The government of Erivan has control over internal affairs, while foreign affairs, the army and certain other departments, are controlled by Moscow. In 1925, 64 per cent of the trade was in private hands and the rest in those of government trading organizations. The government aims at reversing this position of affairs and getting control of 64 per cent of the trade. The governments of Erivan, Tiflis and Baku are quite well aware that if they are to have real autonomy in the future they will have to work hard to lay the foundations of industrial capacity and a stable social life.

Individually the members of the government at Erivan are serious, intelligent and hard-working men; it was a common sight to see these commissars sitting in cold, fireless rooms with their overcoats on, while the available fuel was reserved for heating the larger rooms of their staffs. We met Miasnikian, who was then undoubtedly the most important man in Armenia. He was a typical Russian Armenian, clad in a tunic buckled in at the waist, his hair cropped close. He made his reputation first in Russia by organising resistance to Kolchak. He did fine work in Trans-Caucasia by organizing a stout resistance to the famine.

At the time of my visit Mr Mravian was commissar for foreign affairs. He it was who dealt with us over the question of the 7000 refugees brought to Armenia from Baghdad by the British government. The Lord Mayor's

Fund received the sum of £45,000 for the settlement of these people at Gamarlou [Artashat]. They were successfully established under the general direction of our very capable administrators, the Revd H. W. Harcourt and Mr Dudley S. Northcote.

We saw something of Yerzinkian, commissar for agriculture, and of [Sarkis] Lukashin, now, in 1926, the president. The group of men who threw Armenia into the arms of Russia in the winter of 1920–21 undoubtedly did a real service to their country; at a great cost, no doubt – and at the sacrifice of many cherished traditions and ambitions, and in defiance of public opinion in Europe. Yet it is true that they saved their country from extinction, by the only means available. And whatever the motives of Russia may have been in resuming control over her former Caucasian provinces, it remains undeniable that by so doing she has done more for the Armenians than all the western powers together ... [7]

The Armenians have a capacity to make a great contribution to the world, not only in religion but in art, science and literature. We are inclined to associate Armenia with tragedy and misfortune. Inevitably! Yet there is plenty of evidence of what these people can create when they are given the chance. Even in England where the Armenian community is a small one the public is well acquainted with the work of Sarkis Katchadourian, whose pictures have been so highly praised by Brangwyn; of Haig Gudenian, whose compositions have delighted the Queen's Hall; of Zabelle Boyajian, whose beautiful book *Armenian Legends and Poems* is illustrated with her own drawings. Many other names might be mentioned. Armenian art has its origin in the intoxicating atmosphere of ancient Asia, and for this reason it is infused sometimes with slow and gentle melancholy, sometimes with a delicious rapture which suggests the marvellous moonlight, the wondrous dawn and glorious sunsets of the east. But along with these characteristics there is also a moderation, a logical clearness and a practical element in Armenian thought which marks it as distinctively akin to the western. The Armenians, escaping the cruder forms of fatalism, are inoculated through and through with the doctrine of freedom, and this conviction has never failed to influence their artistic and literary work.[8]

DUDLEY NORTHCOTE

The Revd Dudley Stafford Northcote (1891–1955) was the grandson of the Victorian Tory statesman, Sir Stafford Northcote, (chancellor of the exchequer in 1874–80, and later 1st Earl of Iddesleigh). His father, Amyas Stafford Northcote, was a JP in Buckinghamshire, and his mother was a Southern Belle, Helen May Dudley, of Frankfort, Kentucky. In the first world war, he served as lieutenant with the Ox and Bucks in the Mesopotamian army. After the war, he worked with enormous dedication for Armenian refugees, first in Iraq and then in Soviet Armenia. On his return to England, he took holy orders, and was appointed curate then vicar of St Luke's, Bermondsey (1928–46). Subsequently he became rector of Upton Pyne, near Exeter, from 1946 until his death. His life appears to have been dedicated to the service of others.

A letter home, written a month after the armistice, expresses lively youthful enthusiasm for his new job:

3 December 1918

My dear Mamma,

I am afraid I missed writing the last two weeks, but I have been most awfully busy. In the first place I have left the regiment temporarily and have got quite a new job altogether! I am at present in a place called Bagunba [Baqubah], 30 miles north-east of Baghdad up the Diala river, and I am looking after Armenian refugees. I have 1300 of them to look after and a staff of 5 British Tommies to help. There are heaps more refugees than this, but each batch of 1300 or so has an officer and 5 men to look after it. Things are getting more organized now, but for the last fortnight or so we have been very busy settling down.

This is quite a change from soldiering as you may imagine, and it is not quite the job I would have cared to have during the war, but now that we have absolutely finished active service, I am very pleased to have got it as it is really rather interesting. If you are an ordinary regimental officer with a British regiment, it is astonishing how little opportunity you have of getting to know anything about the natives of Messpot, because of course all your work is with your own men, but now it is part of my job to study 1300 Armenians, men, women and children.[9]

Northcote's contract of service was short-term; in February 1919 he wrote saying that he had signed on for another year of service with the refugees. All the time the belief seemed to be current that the refugees would soon return home, to the Lake Van region, which was their native soil. Like all peasant/agricultural refugees, these Armenians wanted first and foremost to return home, to their own towns and villages. If they returned home, he would too. But no move was made to allow them to go home, so he stayed, working and living with them. By July 1919 he was able to note: 'I can now speak Armenian quite well!' For a year he worked in the camp; then, following a nationalist revolt in Iraq, the camp had to move to Nahr Umar, near Basra. A friend of Dudley Northcote's, W. R. Ward, of the Imperial Bank of Persia, visited the camp in January 1921, and wrote an account of it in a letter to Dudley's mother. The British, Ward said, had devised 'a wonderfully successful way of controlling 13,000 people'.

After breakfast Dudley took me all round the camp. First we went to the orphans' camp in which I think there were 500 children, and these are looked after by paid supervisors from the adults' camp. They are clothed by collections made by the Armenians of Baghdad, who have also sent a few schoolmasters. Dudley persuaded them to do their national dances and sing. Then we went on through the various camps of 1000 each and then to the bazaar. It was all most awfully interesting and wonderfully primitive.[10]

In the summer of 1921 Dudley resigned, and went to work in the refugee camp in Yerevan, where he stayed until 1923, forming a working relationship with the commissars. He enjoyed travelling through the country, and exploring the ancient churches. He visited the Catholicos, and spoke to him without an interpreter. The monastery of Echmiadzin, with its wide courtyards, reminded him of Trinity College, Cambridge. The services in the cathedral were often of three hours' duration, and there were no seats.

The last of his letters is to Mr Carlisle, an official of the Lord Mayor's Fund. It was written from Moscow in February 1923, and is an optimistic summary of the work which had been achieved.

Everything is quite all right in Transcaucasia. I will give you a short summary of what we did during January and of our present position.

Apart from the 600 children that we are keeping at Erivan and Kamarlu we also continued to feed just over 2000 in our country feeding stations. These are distributed as follows:

| | |
|---|---|
| Erivan | 1000 |
| Kamarlu | 200 |
| Echmiadzin | 300 |
| Oushakan | 100 |
| Ashtarak | 250 |
| Bashgarni | 200 |
| | 2050 |

These are still being fed at the present moment. I think we should continue this feeding until April 1st anyhow, and after that it might well be cut out, as by that time the spring will have arrived and with it possibilities of more work and employment with improved conditions in consequence.

We retain the 17 poorest women and girls in our sewing rooms and the 15 poorest lace-makers ... We have ceased altogether to give relief to adult men, and the road-making has been stopped.

We retain the two gardens. Work can shortly recommence in them and it will pay us to keep them. We can pay the necessary labour employed in them with supplies, such as flour and soup. They will produce much valuable food in the way of fresh vegetables for the orphanages.

There is no doubt that the situation in Armenia is much improved owing to the large quantities of flour that have been imported into the country from Russia. This is being sold very cheaply by the Russian State Bank.

We have enough rations on hand to be able to continue the Mesopotamian and Tabriz refugees until the end of June. We still have between £4000 and £5000 left to spend. A medical mission to fight malaria is about the best way to spend it.[11]

In another letter, Northcote had indicated that he was no gloomy, duty-bound worker: 'I am keeping very fit,' he wrote cheerfully, 'and manage to extract quite a lot of enjoyment out of life even in Erivan.'[12]

Soviet communism protected the Armenian people from Turkism; this much was clear to Englishmen such as Buxton and Northcote. Moreover, despite its internationalist posture, communism built up a nation in Soviet Armenia from individuals and groups of widely differing geographical origins. The power to withstand, and the sense of nationhood, have to be balanced against the totalitarianism and Stalinism which were part of the state ideology, although less visible at the start.

Common experiences too welded the nation together: the sense of loss, with all of western and some of eastern Armenia gone, as well as Karabagh and Nakhichevan. The country also endured terrible times of collectivization and purge, and during the second world war Armenia sacrificed a higher than average proportion of its population in the war with Hitler. This was however the time of the beginning of unity with sections of the Armenian diaspora, when donations from Armenians abroad paid for a tank corps which fought the Nazis in the north Caucasus. In 1945 the communist leadership took the important step of rehabilitating the Catholicosate of All Armenians, in Echmiadzin, which had been ignobly degraded during the 1930s.

In the post-war years the Armenian people became unified around their culture, their history, and their industrialized, hard-working country. They grew proud of Yerevan, rebuilt in the 1960s, in which was situated a great manuscript library (the Madenataran), and of the fact that their capital was the oldest city in the USSR. They were grateful, after 1965, to be able to remember the victims of the genocide, with the building of a stark memorial just outside Yerevan.

But by the late 1980s such elements began to lose their power as unifiers of the nation – or perhaps as national symbols (although more real and tangible than symbols) which made communist totalitarianism bearable. Communism became an exhausted bureaucracy, its political programme reduced to little more than corrupt self-perpetuation for the bosses. There had to be massive change, for which the situation of the

Armenians of Mountainous Karabagh became the catalyst. The second republic of Armenia as seen by Smith, Buxton and Northcote had played a valid part. It had created the conditions for survival and progress, although inherent in the communist system were elements of violence and excess which might threaten survival. The condition of Armenians during the last months of communism saw a paradox: the people confident and uncowed, the legacy of Armenian values allowed to flourish by the regime, though often despite its own rhetoric; something that the English charitable workers had worked alongside at the outset. But the politics of the rulers remained locked in a neo-Stalinist mould, the antithesis of the new Armenian woman and man.

## CHAPTER 18

# 'Between Three Worlds and An Adherent of None'
## Philip Marsden in New Armenia

As communism was crumbling in the early 1990s, Philip Marsden, one of a new generation of travellers, undertook a journey in search of Armenia's history, culture, landscape and elusive inner life. While there he was a witness to the process of political dissolution and change. *The Crossing Place*, the superb account of his travels to the heart of Armenia, is a work of rare and sensitive feeling for place and history. It was published in 1993. It belongs to the tradition, which began with *The Preacher's Travels*, of works by British travellers who have spent time among the Armenian people, and recorded what they saw and felt. Marsden explored not just geographic Armenia, but also Armenian diaspora communities in distant lands. One of the most original aspects of his journey is its quest for the communities in Bulgaria and Romania. But perhaps the most memorable part of the book is that which describes life in the homeland itself, especially at the edge of the skirmishes in the war over Nagorno Karabagh. Here too our traveller, like Byron, moved between poetic recollection and the bitter reality of war and change.

Marsden ended his Armenian journey by visiting Tatev, the ninth–thirteenth century monastery in the Zangezur mountains, terrain which is very similar to that of Nagorno Karabagh. Monasteries set amid mountains carry great significance for Armenians: here the faith, language and culture of the nation could be assured of continuity, while invading hordes overran the lowlands. Marsden visited it after a fearsome night of drinking home-made arak.

> Around each of the houses, every inch of space was planted with something edible. There were rows of sprouting potato and cabbage plants and gauntlets of hazel poles waiting for the beans; almond trees and walnut trees hovered over them, between cherry and apple trees. The soil itself was black and sticky, peeled back from the seed-trenches like asphalt. This black soil and its properties are honoured in the name of Karabagh – a Persian–Turkic compound meaning 'Black garden'. It has made these

mountain villages into little Edens, and some of its fecundity has rubbed off on to the villagers themselves, helping to swell their high spirits.

The spirit of Tatev's monastery is more measured. At its centre was the church of Peter and Paul, built at the end of the ninth century. It had the usual genius of form and proportion – the grey flanks of its drum curving with elephantine grace, the threads of its interlacing perfectly spun. I climbed some stone steps and followed the upper walkway out to a grassy rooftop. Dozens of khachkars paraded in the undergrowth; others leaned against each other by the walls, stacked like gifts at the feet of some fabulous potentate. At the edge of the rooftop, the monastery fell away into space. The whole place had been built straight up from the cliff.

I imagined the first monks here, choosing the site. Here they had water and the sound of the water from the falls; they had distant mountains – not so much mountains as peaks; here too were rocks and bands of rocks, cliffs, outcrops, pinnacles and crags, and where there were no rocks there were scrub trees and wide shelves of high grass and the scars of red poppies. This was Armenia, the essential Armenia; it did my hangover no end of good.

At the foot of the cliffs, perhaps seven, eight hundred feet below, amidst a jumble of rocks, I could make out the rectangular compound of another church. Walking down there, on an old path that swung back and forth across the steep slope, it became gradually hotter and more humid, the grass grew higher and the flowers brighter and even more exotic. The air thickened and filled with fat, drowsy bees, and dancing fritillaries flitted among them. Dragonflies hovered over the brooks like airborne crosses. Jays screeched from the elder bushes. The purring of the cicadas became a clamour. Tiny frogs hopped away at my approach, splashing into mossy pools. At one point a metre or so of yellow–green snake flashed across the path, as surprised at my footfalls as I was by its legless wriggling. A few old khachkars were propped up to back on to the gorge, and snails crawled through their weathered fretwork. I took off my coat and carried on.

The church inside was cool and musty. It was deserted and clearly hadn't been used for years. The sun fell through the slit windows in a series of silvery shafts. The walls were maculated with mould, and ferns sprouted from damp crevices. Outside I found a man squatting on a piece of broken cornice. A long grass stem arced from his mouth. I asked him for water and he spun the grass stem but did not move. I told him who I was and what I was doing, and that I was not a Russian and that I needed water. He smiled, then jumped down and led me back through the church.

The man lived alone in the old narthex. His only possession was a broken trunk. From this he produced lavash bread and cheese, and some water and a small bottle of arak. He had fifty hives scattered over the grassy roofs of the monastery, and we ate honey on the lavash that was full of insects and small sticks.

I thanked him and pushed on into the gorge. To get to the road, I had to wade through the river. I walked barefoot down to the bridge and there sat watching the point far above where the road dipped suddenly from the plateau and started its long, hairpinning descent. A black dot appeared and it took another fifteen minutes before it reached the bridge. The door opened and there in the back, in dark glasses and a perfectly pressed cassock, was the bishop of Goris.

The bishop gave me a lift out of the gorge and dropped me off on the main road south. I waited an hour before the next car came through. The Papazian family, or at least a part of it, was on its way home to Ghapan. They had been to a wedding. Baron Papazian drove with intense concentration; his breath smelt of arak and he had difficulty in focusing on the road. Mother and daughter wore their smartest frocks, one a black and yellow print, the other black and mauve; When we stopped at a spring in the forest, they tottered through the mud like a pair of tropical birds.

These springs were a part of every Armenian journey. I had been on buses which had stopped simply so that people could visit a certain spring, filing up like liturgants to take the water. Many of the churches were built near water, no doubt replacing earlier sites of worship. Water held a peculiar significance for Armenians. (And I thought suddenly of the marches in the desert and no water, and those other springs at Ras ul-Ain and the desert cisterns choked with corpses ...) Here the water was channelled into a pipe which pushed through a large stone. At the foot of the stone was a trough and the water slopped constantly over the rim of the trough to drain away down a gully. Above the pipe was chiselled, as at so many springs I had seen, the now familiar circle of spinning segments. The two Papazian ladies dabbed water on their rouged cheeks before returning to the car.

But as we pulled up out of the shadows of the forest, refreshed and watered, another car flashed past us. We all saw its shattered rear window and the man lolling across the back seat.

Baron Papazian tightened his lips. 'Last night they killed a man on this road. I think maybe we will not get through.'

Sure enough, cresting a hill, we came across two or three cars and a bus stopped on the road. A crowd milled around it, dwarfed by the presence of some anxious looking fedayi. They propped their Kalashnikovs against their hips. There'd been an ambush on the road ahead. But in their excitement no one could tell me more. All that I could make out was: 'Russian! Mussulman!' The Papazian family said they could not risk it and would head back to Goris. I thanked them and said I'd wait. Maybe the bus would get through later; this was the only road south.

The forest was set back from the road and there was a meadow of poppies and high grass. The poppies looked like spots of blood in the glade. In the distance beneath the southern sky was a line of dusty grey peaks, the last peaks of Armenia.

I paced up and down the road. Ever since I'd plotted my journey, poring over maps in Jerusalem, I'd assumed that the Araxes river and the Iranian border would be its end. Getting to the bottom of Armenia was the journey's motif, its pattern and, physically at least, the bottom of Armenia was the southern border and the river. But what could the maps tell me of this?

The fedayi advised people to return to Goris. But I waited, unable to believe I would be thwarted here. Several hours later a truck pulled into the clearing; it would be going through. I hauled myself up into the cab.

The road to Ghapan was paved with past incursions. Strange burnt-out buildings stood among the trees. The airport on the edge of the town was a wreck. Approaching the narrow end of the republic, the far end of Armenia, I had the sense of something frayed, like the sleeve of an old shirt or a flag left out too long in the wind. Ghapan itself was a confused and broken town. An abandoned fun-fair lay rusting in its centre. The streets were full of swaying Armenians. Their faces would loom out of the dusk. The government hotel was still just about functioning. Having gone through the well-rehearsed routine of explaining that I was not Russian, and how I'd got to Armenia, and the countries I'd been through, the Armenians I'd met, they awarded me the Party Suite. There was no question of payment.

With the door closed I fell exhausted into one of the tobacco-brown armchairs. Guiltily I thought of all the communists who'd lolled in this seat before me. I thought of their good intentions, and their fat, shiny-suited behinds, their moustachioed self-importance. Then I fell asleep. Shortly before midnight I woke and pushed open the bathroom door. Something green-and-white slithered across the tiled floor. It disappeared into a large hole in the wall before I could make out what it was. Throughout the night there was a series of bangs that reverberated faintly through the walls. I was awake a long time trying to decide whether it was the green-and-white beast, the plumbing, or artillery raining down from the hills.

In the morning I phoned the local priest. He said he had benzine and would be going south that day and could give me a lift. We drove over a pass in cloud, but by the time we reached the town of Meghri it was hot and dry.

Meghri was an oppressive place. Not a moment went by when I wasn't aware of some sense of encroachment. On all sides the mountains loomed over the town – bare, treeless mountains with sharp ridges which were either in shadow or else a constantly changing backdrop of blues and yellows and reds. There was an unfamiliar dryness to the place. Looking across the gorge, across the wire, to the dragon's teeth ridges of Iran, I felt the vastness of the east and, by contrast, the last squashed-up corner of Armenia. But it was, as ever, the unseen, human threat that weighed heaviest in Meghri. Azerbaijan lay ten miles away, both to the east and to the west. Soviet tanks were dotted along the frontier and to the north, between the people of Meghri and their compatriots, lay nine thousand feet of mountain. Meghri is Armenia in miniature, isolated and exposed: Armenia on the border, between Iranian Shiites, Turkish Sunnis and the rags of Soviet communism, between three worlds and an adherent of none.[1]

# REFERENCES

## 1. ANTIQUITY AND THE MIDDLE AGES

1. T. Rymer, *Foedera*, The Hague, 1739–45 edition, vol. I, part iii, p. 204
2. ibid., I, iv, pp. 113, 114
3. ibid., I, iv, p. 114
4. ibid., I, iv, p. 110
5. ibid., II, iii, p. 139
6. ibid., III, i, p. 200
7. ibid., III, ii, p. 85
8. *Chronique du religieux de St Denis*, Paris, 1839, vol. I, p. 421
9. Rymer, *Foedera*, III, iii, p. 186
10. J. Froissart, *Chronicles*, (T. Johnes, trans.), 1844, vol. II, p. 199
11. Rymer, *Foedera*, III, iii, p. 186
12. *Chronique du religieux*, I, 425
13. Holinshed, *Chronicle*, London, 1807 edition, vol. II, p. 768
14. Rymer, *Foedera*, III, iii, p. 192
15. ibid., III, iv, p. 38
16. John Gower, *Confessio Amantis*, book IV, 1245–504
17. Quoted in James Bryce, *Transcaucasia and Ararat*, 4th edition, 1896, pp. 218–20

## 2. 'A PEOPLE VERY INDUSTROUS IN ALL KIND OF LABOUR'

1. John Cartwright, *The Preacher's Travels* ..., Harleian Collection, 1745, vol. I, p. 720
2. ibid., p. 721
3. ibid., p. 723
4. ibid., p. 724
5. ibid., pp. 724–5
6. John Fryer, *A New Account of East India and Persia* ...,1688, Hakluyt Society reprint, London, 1912, vol. II, p. 209
7. ibid., p. 249
8. ibid., p. 259
9. ibid., pp. 261–2
10. ibid., pp. 277–82

## 3. 'THE THEATRE OF PERPETUAL WAR'

1. Jonas Hanway, *The Revolutions of Persia*, 1762 edition, vol. II, pp. 160–2
2. ibid., p. 163
3. ibid., p. 252
4. Edward Gibbon, *The History of the Decline and Fall of the Roman Empire*, Everyman edition, 1910 and reprints, vol. V, chapter 47, pp. 61–2
5. ibid., chapter 54, p. 497
6. ibid., pp. 499–501


## 4. 'IT WAS IN ARMENIA THAT PARADISE WAS PLACED'

1. Lord Byron, *Works*, E. H. Coleridge (ed.), London, 1899, Poetry, vol. II, p. 192
2. ibid., p. 191
3. ibid., *Childe Harold*, II, lxxiv
4. ibid., lxxvi
5. Byron, *Letters and Journals*, Leslie Marchand (ed.), London, 1976, vol. V, p. 137
6. ibid., pp. 130–1
7. ibid., p. 152
8. ibid., p. 156
9. ibid., p. 157n
10. ibid., vol. IX, p. 31
11. Byron, *Letters and Journals*, R. E. Prothero (ed.), London, 1900, vol. IV, pp. 429–33
12. *Lord Byron's Armenian Exercises and Poetry*, Venice (S. Lazzaro), 1870, pp. 33–5


## 5. 'A VAST SOLITUDE ON THE GREY AND WINTRY PLAIN'

1. Sir Robert Ker Porter, *Travels in Georgia, Persia, Armenia and Ancien Babylon*, London, 1821, vol. I, pp. 172–5
2. Richard Wilbraham, *Travels in Trans-Caucasian Provinces of Russia*, London, 1839, pp. 286–7
3. ibid., p. 351
4. ibid., p. 332
5. James Brant, 'Notes of a journey through a Part of Kurdistan, in the Summer of 1838', *Journal of the Royal Geographical Society*, 10, 1841, pp. 398–400


## 6. 'A HEALTHY AND A HARDY RACE'

1. James Morier, *A Second Journey Through Persia, Armenia and Asia Minor, to Constantinople, between the Years 1810 and 1816*, London, 1818, pp. 323–4
2. ibid., p. 326
3. ibid., p. 304
4. ibid., p. 312
5. ibid., p. 337
6. ibid., p. 341

7. Sarah Searight, *The British in the Middle East*, London, 1969, pp. 181–2

8. James Morier, *The Adventures of Hajji Baba of Ispahan*, popular edition, London, c. 1899, pp. 168–209


7. 'WOULD THAT YOU WOULD LOVE ME'

1. George Borrow, *Lavengro*, Constable edition, London, 1923, vol. I, pp. 445–53

2. ibid., vol. II, pp. 1–4

3. ibid., p. 331

4. ibid., p. 16

5. George Borrow, *The Romany Rye*, Constable edition, London, 1923, vol. I, pp. 145–50


8. 'THE GROANING AND COMPLAINING OF NEIGHBOURING QUADRUPEDS'

1. Archibald Forbes et al., *The War Correspondence of the Daily News*, vol. II, London, 1878, pp. 124, 127–30


9. 'A CONSCIOUSNESS OF SOME HEAVY RESPONSIBILITY'

1. 'E. J. Dillon' (d. 1933), in *Dictionary of National Biography*

2. *Chester Chronicle*, 10 August 1895, p. 6

3. *Liverpool Daily Post*, 25 September 1896, p. 6

4. ibid.

5. George Douglas Campbell, Duke of Argyll, *Our Responsibilities for Turkey: Facts and Memories of Forty Years*, London, 1896, pp. 32–3

6. ibid., p. 61

7. ibid., p. 68

8. ibid., p. 74

9. ibid., p. 84

10. ibid., pp. 81–2, 121

11. ibid., pp. 146–8

12. Hansard, *Commons*, vol. XXXVIII, 3 March 1896, col. 75

13. ibid., cols. 83–5

14. William Watson, *The Purple East*, London, 1896, p. 35

15. ibid., p. 29


10. THE KEY OF TRUTH

1. F. C. Conybeare (ed. and trans.) *The Key of Truth: a Manual of the Paulician Church of Armenia*, Oxford, 1898, p. xxxi

2. ibid., p. lxxii

3. ibid., p. lxxv

4. ibid., p. 75

5. ibid., p. 111

## 11. 'TO STRENGTHEN AN ANCIENT CHURCH'

1. Archdeacon E. Dowling, *The Armenian Church*, London, 1910, p. 149
2. Lambeth Palace Papers, Jerusalem and the East Mission File, file 2330

## 12. 'AT THE MOON'S INN'

1. Mrs Isabella Bishop, *Journeys in Persia and Kurdistan*, London, 1891 and reprint, vol. I, p. 269
2. ibid., pp. 269–70
3. ibid., pp. 270–1
4. ibid., pp. 271–2
5. ibid., vol. II, pp. 341–2
6. ibid., p. 373
7. ibid., p. 374
8. ibid., p. 385
9. Lucy Garnett, *Turkish Life in Town and Country*, London, 1904, pp. 176–82

## 13. 'A VAST DOME OF SNOW'

1. H. F. B. Lynch, *Armenia: Travels and Studies*, London, 1901, reprinted Beirut, 1965, vol. I, pp. 93–4
2. ibid., p. 142
3. ibid., pp. 149–52
4. ibid., pp. 153–4
5. ibid., vol. II, pp. 35–7
6. ibid., pp. 191–3
7. ibid., p. 382

## 14. 'WHY HAS THE TIDE OF CIVILIZATION PAUSED?'

1. Arnold Toynbee, 'Sir Edwin Pears', *Dictionary of National Biography*
2. Sir Edwin Pears, *Turkey and its People*, London, 1911, pp. 270–2
3. ibid., pp. 275–6
4. Noel and Harold Buxton, *Travels and Politics in Armenia*, London, 1914, pp. 140–4

## 15. 'ABSOLUTELY PREMEDITATED AND SYSTEMATIC'

1. *The Times* (London), 10 November 1916, p. 10, col. 3
2. Hansard, *Lords*, 28 July 1915, vol. XIX, cols. 774–8
3. ibid., 6 October 1915, cols. 1000–2
4. ibid., col. 1004
5. Hansard, *Commons*, 16 November 1915, vol. LXXV, cols. 1761–4
6. ibid., col. 1764

7. Great Britain, Parliamentary Papers, Miscellaneous No. 31 (1916), p. xxix; also published with the title The *Treatment of Armenians in the Ottoman Empire*, London, 1916; reprinted with decoding appendix, Beirut, 1972

8. ibid., p. xxxi

9. ibid., p. xxxii

10. ibid., pp. 593–653

11. ibid., p. 627

12. ibid., pp. 627–32

13. ibid., p. 633


## 16. 'A STABLE AND CIVILIZING FORCE'

1. W. E. D. Allen, 'The Armenians: Their Past and Their Future', *Quarterly Review*, 233 (January/April 1920), pp. 237–44

2. ibid., p. 240

3. ibid., pp. 242–4

4. W. E. D. Allen and Paul Muratoff, *Caucasian Battlefields*, Cambridge, 1953, pp. 458–9

5. ibid., pp. 461–2

6. ibid., p. 469

7. ibid., pp. 469–70

8. ibid., pp. 475–6


## 17. 'TO REGAIN THEIR SELF-RESPECT BY USEFUL LABOUR'

1. Dr Armstrong Smith, *Famine in Transcaucasia*, London, 1922, p. 4

2. ibid., pp. 13–14

3. ibid., pp. 15–16

4. ibid., pp. 18–19

5. ibid., pp. 19–20

6. ibid., pp. 22–3

7. Harold Buxton, *Trans-Caucasia*, London, 1926, pp. 54–6

8. ibid., pp. 57–8

9. British Library, Northcote Papers, Add. Ms. 57559, 1/1

10. ibid., 1/8

11. ibid., 2/5

12. ibid., 3/18


## 18 'BETWEEN THREE WORLDS AND AN ADHERENT OF NONE'

1. Philip Marsden, *The Crossing Place*, London, 1993, pp. 230–5

## FURTHER READING

The bibliography is extensive. This brief list is no more than a guide to
further reading, and it excludes the texts noted as sources. Readers seeking
a more thorough survey of the field will find useful references in the
bibliographies of H. F. B. Lynch's *Armenia: Travels and Studies* (1901), and
in the volumes (noted below) by Professor Hovannisian. There are many
titles listed in Dr A. Salmaslian's *Bibliographie de l'Arménie* (Paris, 1946,
revised edition, Yerevan, 1969).

Anderson, M. S., *The Eastern Question 1774–1923*, London, 1966

Carswell, John, *New Julfa: The Armenian Churches and Other Buildings*, Oxford,
1968

Der Nersessian, S., *The Armenians*, London, 1969

Hovannisian, Richard G., *The Republic of Armenia*, 4 vols., Los Angeles,
1971–96

Lang, David Marshall, *Armenia: Cradle of Civilization*, London, 1970

Nassibian, Akaby, *Britain and the Armenian Question 1915–1923*, London, 1984

Somakian, Manoug. J., *Empires in Conflict: Armenia and the Great Powers 1895–
1920*, London, 1996

Walker, Christopher J., *Armenia: the Survival of a Nation*, London, 1990

 INDEX